How will you reach your next summit?

REACHING YOUR NEXT SUMMIT!

9 Vertical Lessons for Leading with Impact

Manley Feinberg II

INDIE BOOKS
INTERNATIONAL

ISBN-10: 1-941870-68-6
ISBN-13: 978-1-941870-68-6
Library of Congress Control Number: 2016952727

Designed by Joni McPherson, www.mcphersongraphics.com

Cover photo: Manley gunning for the summit of El Capitan on "Tangerine Trip", September 2013. Photo by Chris West, VideoNarrative.com

Section Photos: Rich Copeland looking to his Next Summit on the Southwest Face of El Capitan. Photo by Logan Talbott.

Back Cover photo by Keith Lee, KeithLeeStudios.com

All other photos by Manley Feinberg II

INDIE BOOKS INTERNATIONAL, LLC
2424 VISTA WAY, SUITE 316
OCEANSIDE, CA 92054

www.indiebooksintl.com

PRAISE FOR *REACHING YOUR NEXT SUMMIT*

"*Manley's Vertical Lessons have made a significant impact on me, our organization and our customers. He has written a business and personal leadership book that is truly exceptional. The narrative is intensely engaging, worth a read on its own. Not only that, the insights he puts in your hands are easy to implement and will help you climb from where you are, to your vision of what's possible. Put this book in the hands of your people and you will be better for it.*"
Vance Brown, Executive Chairman and Co-founder of Cherwell Software, author of *No Matter the Cost*

"Reaching Your Next Summit! *gives us an inspiring inside view of Manley Feinberg's truly extraordinary journeys toward life's summits. His fascinating stories range from one of climbing to rarely-reached heights in remote Kyrgyzstan, to one of leaving a longstanding corporate leadership role to pursue his passion for speaking—actions that may seem equally out of reach to most of us. With authenticity and heart, Manley inspires us to deeply reflect, reconsider perceived limits, and take action to reach our own personal summits, however out of reach they may seem. This is a book that impacts life and leadership, at work and at home.*"
Laurie Ferrendelli, Director of Organizational Development at Barry-Wehmiller Companies, Inc.

"Reaching Your Next Summit! *is a captivating cliff hanger with real life experiences translated into mind, heart, and soul inspired lessons. Anyone searching for inspiration, motivation, and encouragement to reach beyond the obstacles holding them back must read this book. You will not be able to put this book down from the moment you open it.*"
Daryl Pint, CEO of Ceva Biomune

"*This book isn't just about leadership and breaking barriers. It's about heart. It's about grit. It's about tapping into the core of who you are to find the greatness that lies within. Anyone looking to scale the next summit in their life should read this book.*"
Lt. Col. Rob "Waldo" Waldman, New York Times bestselling author of *Never Fly Solo*

"*I found this book captivating, the lessons both powerful and immediately accessible. After a lifetime of sales and leadership experience, I can say this is a book that will make a difference in the hands of your people. Your sales teams will see the way to building more meaningful relationships and gain clarity to reach the summit of the mountains your business is climbing. Every person who reads it will be both inspired and equipped to bring their best to life everyday. Read it and you will be rewarded.*"
Andreas Buhr, entrepeneur, speaker and author

"Reaching Your Next Summit! *will help you drive ROI for your business and life! I was mesmerized and completely engaged by Manley's writing style from start to finish. I found his principles fully aligned with strategies and tactics that I have seen develop and grow strategic partnerships for decades. This is an exceptional work that will help you climb the mountains of life, and achieve more.*"
Ed Rigsbee, Author of *Developing Strategic Alliances*

"*Amazing. And beautiful. Manley's genuine spirit and soul bring an inspired journey for all leaders to breathe in, contemplate, and put into action. With a scenic backdrop, walls to scale, and Manley as your guide—you will be embracing your new summit! On belay!*"
Julie L. Mohr, International Speaker and Author

"*Are you wanting to thrive in your business and life and ultimately find the pinnacle of joy and success? Practicing the right skills not only gets you there, it is mandatory. In* Reaching Your Next Summit! *Manley uses his experience in mountain climbing and the business world to give us practical lessons we can implement now. He lays the foundation required for entrepreneurs, career decisions, or life aspirations throughout every chapter. It's a must read for any leader who wants to stand on their next summit."*

Mike Kublin, President of People Tek and author of *12 Steps For Courageous Leadership: Start your Journey now!*

"In this book Manley Feinberg does a great job of reminding us all that anything is possible when you lead with gratitude and speak heart to heart. In each Vertical Lesson he spells out how leaders can reach their next summit."

Thom Singer, author of *Some Assembly Required: How to Make, Grow and Keep your Business Relationships*

"A mind-blowing metaphorical journey into the world of practical leadership, wisdom and application. With so many books and perspectives in this paradigm it can be difficult for potential readers to determine where they should endeavor their time. Manley craftily takes you by the hand onto the ledges of a pulsating journey which engages you to re-define and re-articulate a strategic vision on both a personal and business level. On Belay Manley...and a most sincere thank you for your brilliance and ultimate sophistication to tackle such a misunderstood principle. Your metaphor pours across the pages and impacts the reader whether they are in a boardroom, parenting, coaching or working in a business environment. I can't wait for the next book. A great book's influence is never neutral. Manley pushed this theory into overdrive."

Mark Maloney, CEO Maloney Global Group of Companies

"Feinberg's Reaching Your Next Summit! *weaves page-turning personal climbing narrative with astute and insightful Vertical Lessons, a must read for those who want to lead with integrity and thrive in today's uncertain environment."*

Matt Walker, author of *Adventure in Everything*

"Vertical Lessons provides inspiring, thought provoking insights and examples on how to be a better leader and teammate. Things we can all do to lead from wherever we are."
Phil Gerbyshak, leadership and sales expert, author of Leadership Gone Social

"Reaching Your Next Summit! is unlike other leadership books. It challenged me. It made me uncomfortable. And it was exhilarating! Read this and take your life and business to the next level."
Stephen Shapiro, author of Best Practices are Stupid

"You don't need to be a leader, climber, or have a title to benefit from this book. I could not put this book down and have already benefited directly from it in my business and personal life. Page after page is filled with my notes, highlights and personal epiphanies. I am recommending this to all my clients. I don't know of a more effective resource to help those who are ready to grow their business and their personal contribution to the world. Read it. Engage in the simple and effective exercises. Then reflect, and get ready to step onto Your Next Summit!"
Ed Tate, CSP and World Champion of Public Speaking

"I am a goal-driven, purpose driven person and my long-term ambition is to empower others. Manley's Vertical Lessons brought me clarity through his real-life stories, pictures, and words of wisdom. His guidance and lessons are used to answer our doubting questions, 'Is it worth it? What should I do?' Thank you Manley for your ability to motivate others through your personal examples of Vertical Lessons."
Deb Bostic, Senior Vice President and Chief Human Resources Officer, First Bank

"What a great book. Manley Feinberg teaches us how leading others to their success will take us to new levels of success as well. This fun and compelling book is filled with great stories that captivate, teach and show us how to grow."
Sam Silverstein, CSP, author of Non-Negotiable and No More Excuses, Past President, The National Speakers Association

"What an amazing story to help leaders climb to the next level. Manley has used his spectacular adventure to illustrate lessons that every leader should learn. Get your copy and apply these principles today!"
Stephen Tweed, CSP, CEO of Leading Home Care

"Manley has redefined the meaning of reaching your personal peak! His leadership lessons will take you straight to the top with his engaging and practical approach to success. Open your heart and mind and get ready for a life changing experience that will have immediate and lasting effects!"
Jason Young, Founder LeadSmart, Inc., author of *Culturetopia* and former Leadership Development and Customer Service Trainer at Southwest Airlines

"In this smart, fast-moving book, Manley Feinberg lays out your foundations for success in leadership, in business, and in life. Manley takes climbing principles and practices, breaks them down into actionable "do-this-now" steps giving leaders at every level the mindset, skill set, and toolset for lasting impact. If you're looking to upgrade your career, your team, or your organization—look no further. THE leadership book for the rest of us is here. Buy a copy for everyone on your team. Yes, it's that good."
David Newman, CSP, author of *Do It! Marketing*

"This book is a rare work. Part epic mountain adventure, part guidebook to leading a more productive life, it is both engaging and practical. Manley connects in a very personal way and motivates people to step up and lead, regardless of their title. It will help light the fire in you and your employees, and drive the performance you need to impact your bottom line."
Eric Chester, Author of *On Fire At Work: How Great Companies Ignite Passion in Their People Without Burning Them Out*

Table of Contents

Foreword

I was lost in the depth of the Amazon jungle for weeks, bare to the bone, no food, no knife, no fire; one man against the most extreme natural elements, alone. Torrential storms swayed the giant trees, causing them to collapse all around. Flooding rivers chased me in the woods trying to drown me; deadly swamps held me prisoner for long, sticky hours. Jaguars were stalking me day and night, wild boars, venomous snakes, wasps, and parasites; my body was one open wound. I hadn't eaten for days, reduced to skin hanging on bones. My lifelong dream of grandeur and famed adventure had turned into the worst nightmare. It is there that I found myself, and from there I rose, a different man, a hero, for sometimes you must get lost to find yourself.

Maybe this is why we do crazy things.

George Mallory famously said he attempted to climb the Everest because it was there. Mallory never made it to the summit, but he died trying. And so died Colonel Fawcett in his obsession to find Eldorado. The mad longing for the unattainable; insatiable passion; pushing oneself beyond what's possible, just to touch the aloof. An urge that defies rational thinking just as it defies gravitational laws, as it breaks the barriers between the force of nature and the human nature in a holy reunion, making them one and the same.

One cannot conquer a mountain, said Hillary, after his ascent to the Everest, but rather the mountain allows us to conquer ourselves.

And then comes Manley. He knows he cannot subdue a rock. The rock is simply there, ever protruding, omnipresent, deep in its silent contemplation, oblivious. The rock is there, untamable, unbeatable, mute and dumb, indifferent to your desires and efforts.

And yet it is encouraging you, Manley; it inspires you, it dares you, and in its infinite generosity, it allows you to shape your life's meaning against it. No, you don't try to conquer it; it is your fears that you want to meet. It will set your demons free; you will have let go of your pretense before you can soar free like a peregrine. You did it Manley; you broke the limiting shackles of your consciousness that kept you affixed to the ground and anchored your body to the vertical rock, ready to die or to reach the top.

But why did you leave the safety of your home Manley, why did you travel so far beyond the remote prairies of Kyrgyzstan to those hidden valleys? For the same reason I was lost in the depths of the Amazon; you came to live or die here because you knew life is meaningless unless you find yourself. And what an adventure you lived to tell, what a wall you chose to climb; the madness, the passion, the punishment.

Placing your life in the hands of a brooding, epileptic stranger? And in turn holding his life and that of his wife in your tired, blistered hands, on belay? There, on the rock, light-footed as an ibex, you were finally free, and you knew you belonged.

But there, at the summit, like the Buddha, you understood something else. Attaining it for yourself couldn't be the goal. It was sharing "the way" with others that is your true, noble calling.

And we follow you, riveted to your stories, joyously crying at the summit, tragically shedding a tear for the loss of a beloved friend. You use the rocks as metaphors, drawing from their silence the deepest insights that have transformed your life forever and will transform ours as well, if we dare to let go, knowing we've got you on belay.

Yossi Ghinsberg
International best-selling author of *Jungle*

Preface

It was November 3, 2014, in Eau Claire, Wisconsin. I had just wrapped up the first of fifty keynotes to the management team at Menards, the third-largest home improvement retailer in the United States. In the audience was fellow speaker and friend, Bob Phibbs. That evening I was looking forward to the opportunity to get to know Bob, learn how I could support his efforts, and listen carefully to his feedback. I had learned from my father and stepfather in fourth grade that being coachable and seeking feedback from others was an essential key to dramatically speeding up the pace of improvement in any pursuit. I was not seeking validation (although that is helpful to keep the wind in the sails), but I valued Bob's qualified perspective as a successful professional speaker.

We connected for dinner at our hotel, then drove for what felt like an hour to the other side of Eau Claire to the one luxurious steak house in the region to celebrate the day. I'll never forget the single essential question Bob asked me in the first five minutes of dinner. "Manley, I have a pressing question, and I bet that the rest of the audience wants to know too—why do you climb? I don't get it. It looks pretty challenging!"

For the next seventy minutes, I tried my best to explain to Bob what had inspired me to seek out adventure and extraordinary physical challenges in my life. It was a struggle, at best, and I don't think I ever *did* come up with a reasonable explanation. I did, however, stumble up a realization.

I believe the reason I climb is the same reason you may be reading these words right now. That is, you have caught a glimpse of what is possible in one or more areas of your life, and you just can't settle for the way things are anymore.

Have you ever walked into your home after a challenging day and vented your frustrations to a loved one? And then heard this response? "If it is so stressful and challenging, why don't you do something different?"

But you don't quit. You keep coming back to face the challenges.

What is it about challenges that engage us at a deeper level and bring out our very best?

Challenges expose our vulnerabilities, forcing us to examine our weaknesses while leveraging our strengths. Of course, there is always an alternative: stop stepping up to challenging scenarios and accept mediocrity. This is a course taken by many people. I don't believe it is always by deliberate decision, but through a life of choices and circumstance, they find themselves, as Henry David Thoreau said, "leading lives of quiet desperation."

If you believe there is something more, this book is for you. You know a more engaged, fulfilled life is possible, and you believe your work on this earth is not done yet. You can't stand the thought of just coasting under the radar, and are ready to leverage new strategies and tools to help you realize more. More focus, more courage, more commitment, and more momentum to reach your next summit—and beyond.

That is why I climb mountains.

Most of my time is spent climbing the same mountains you are facing, though. Not physical mountains; the challenge of growing my business. The challenge of engaging my team at a deeper level. The challenge of making the personal choice to exercise and eat well. The challenge of ensuring I have enough of my very best to serve my family and friends every day. The challenge of supporting my clients in a way that enriches their lives and helps them achieve their work and life objectives.

When we are able to live life in a way that brings more joy to our time here, and helps us share the best of what we have to give with those who love and need us most, life is good. That's why I climb the physical and day-to-day mountains we face.

I believe the human drive to improve is within us all, calling us to realize more of what is possible. I want to invite you to join me in renewing your commitment to keep climbing, to reach for excellence and to realize more of your potential on this life journey. In the pages that follow, you will learn nine lessons and one essential question from *The Vertical* that will dramatically improve your ability to reach your next summit and beyond.

The Vertical is what I call the realm in climbing where you have left behind the comfort and security of your day-to-day horizontal existence. You have sharpened your focus and committed to something worth reaching for. In The Vertical, the more you *embrace the exposure*, the more you thrive.

If you choose to implement these lessons in your life, I can confidently promise you three things:

ONE: You will master the *Art of the Restart*, and you will realize more momentum.

TWO: You will learn to battle emotional gravity every day in the small choices you make between *what is* and *what could be*.

THREE: You will see intangible and tangible results in your life.

Enhance your experience:

I invite you to visit ReachingYourNextSummit.com for free resources, full color photos and video to enrich your experience with this book.

〰 Access to free content updates, templates, and exercises

〰 Vertical Lessons Strategic Summary PDF

〰 Full color photos and videos

〰 Visit ReachingYourNextSummit.com

Get On Belay with Manley:
Human Voice: 314-724-3443
Manley@VerticalLessons.com

Manley Feinberg II
Vertical Lessons, Inc.
816 Aldan Dr.
St. Louis, MO. 63132

SECTION ONE
Why Climb?

CHAPTER 1

The Call to Reach Your Next Summit

The seed was planted in my mind in the fall of 1997. As I opened an issue of *Rock and Ice* magazine, I was swept away into a mysterious and remote corner of the world. The 20-page special report was about a country whose terrain was more than 90 percent mountains, most of which had yet to be climbed: Kyrgyzstan, Central Asia. A primary focus of the piece was the Aksu Valley; considered to be one of the last frontiers in "big-wall" climbing, due to the size, magnitude, and incredible number of sheer granite faces in this region.

 Big-wall climbing is a type of rock climbing in which a climber ascends a rock wall so tall that you typically have to live on the sheer vertical face for anywhere from a few days to multiple weeks to reach the summit. Big-wall climbing is often logistically complicated by the need to haul heavy amounts of gear to eat, sleep, and survive in The Vertical, completely self-supported.

In 1983, the first Soviet climbers had entered the Aksu Valley. In 1995, the first American climbers visited as part of the elite North Face Expedition team. Something about that area, as described in that article, captured my spirit more than the typical coverage of the latest hot spot on the planet. I believe it was primarily how it was accurately positioned as the ultimate exotic big-wall climbing destination in the world. So many walls with so much potential. An extraordinary culture in a region that was rich with uncharted opportunity. Of course, there's always a catch. Not only was the region very difficult to access due to its remote location on earth, but the logistics of traveling in the area were further complicated by political instability, corruption at all levels of government, and extensive social disruption fueled by Islamic fundamentalists who were active in the region. This was surely enough to scare me right out of my dream were it not for a serious advantage that developed next.

Less than a month later, I was sitting with my brother, Craig, at lunch in Louisville, Kentucky. He announced a recently materialized opportunity to go to Kyrgyzstan to fight poverty from the ground up through the efforts of microcredit banking. Craig had joined the Peace Corps after college and was on the frontier of microcredit financial development in Third World countries. It has proven to be one of the most effective tools for stimulating and reversing poverty in developing countries. From the villages to even larger cities, people have no means to get small-business loans or even basic resources. This revolutionary approach works by avoiding corrupt governments and the trickle-down flow of traditional aid monies. Microcredit instead flows directly into the hands of those who need it most in the suppressed economic environments.

I remember sitting at the table when Craig enthusiastically described the region and made his invitation official. "Bro, you must come visit and do some climbing! The climbing is way above my skills level, so I won't make a great partner on the walls, but I can help you get there. Regardless of what you climb, we'll have the time of our lives. It's going to be amazing."

For two years I trained, researched, planned, and scraped up money to fund the expedition. My father committed to helping me with my plane ticket, and my fiancé committed to being there when I returned. This allowed me to check off two of my top concerns. There were several obvious questions to answer, and many I'd never even imagined. What mountains would I climb? How would I get there? What was the weather like? What was the nature of the rock in the region? Was a climb even possible for me? Answers to those questions quickly revealed that climbing in Kyrgyzstan would, at best, require skills beyond my current skill set, and without question be way beyond my comfort zone.

Another critical challenge would be to find the right climbing partner.

I knew from past climbing failures and successes that *climbing with incredible partners only* was an essential element for success— but who was going to be willing to go with me to Kyrgyzstan? I tried persuading all of my former partners and friends who were serious climbers, many of whom were professional climbers at that time. Despite my best efforts, I struggled for months to find a partner from the United States to join me and make the epic adventure. Most of my professional climbing friends were not available due to other expedition commitments, and my other friends had an impressive list of reasons and excuses why they couldn't seize this opportunity. Three months before I was due to leave, I still did not have a partner lined up, but other possible options emerged.

My brother made friends with an American climber based in Kyrgyzstan who was interested in climbing with me. This was better than no partner, but not ideal. I had never met "Josh," and had no idea whether he even came close to fitting the profile of my *Incredible-Partner-Only* principle. I had to make a difficult decision. Was I willing to travel halfway around the world without a partner and hope that a someone I had never met might work out?

By this point, I was quite discouraged and overwhelmed at the thought of traveling with 280 pounds of baggage by myself. I decided it was worth a shot. The breakthrough that helped me take the leap was accepting the reality that this was *my only chance* to get over there and possibly climb.

Finally, the moment to leave arrived. July 1, 1999. My fiancé, Emily, made the three-hour drive from Paducah, Kentucky to the St. Louis, Missouri airport. She dropped me off and I hopped on a TWA flight. I landed in Detroit, Michigan, and was held over on the tarmac by a three-hour thunderstorm. This put me into the JFK airport at 11:30 p.m., missing my Turkish Air flight into Istanbul, Turkey the next day.

Little did I know, the challenges were just beginning.

I remember approaching the TWA counter and how callous the agent was. She didn't seem to care that the trip of a lifetime that I had planned for two years was in jeopardy. My heart sank as I listened to her solution. "I've booked you through Moscow in five days; until then, you'll need to find your own hotel and accommodations in New York City while you wait for our next available route into central Asia."

I tried to explain to her that if I didn't make it into central Asia within forty-eight hours, it would completely throw off the tight timeline of my expedition and ruin my entire trip. She had no sympathy whatsoever. "Well, you do have one other option. I can fly you back to St. Louis in the morning—that's it. Take it or leave it."

Great. "I guess I'm going to Moscow."

The walk from that ticket counter to the baggage claim counter one level below was a long sad trudge. I tried to stand patiently in line at the baggage counter where there were three agents working. By the time I got to the front, my face had grown so long and depressed I probably looked as though I had just lost a dear friend.

The baggage agent looked at me and said, "What in the world is wrong with you? You're not having a good day, huh?"

"No. My dream trip has just been completely destroyed."

She asked what I was referring to. I explained.

"I have a dream to go to central Asia to climb. I have been planning for two years and am desperately trying to save this once-in-a-lifetime opportunity. If I do not get out on a flight tonight into Istanbul, there is no way the trip will happen due to the limited flights into central Asia and the logistics of the entire journey."

She turned to her colleague, a gentleman on her left, and started mentioning a few airlines and codes. He jumped on the phone and made two calls. Meanwhile, she and the agent to her right were frantically typing on their keyboards.

Then he hung up the phone, reached down below the counter,

and broke out a little metal lockbox. It was a cash box, maybe 4" tall × 8" wide. You know the type, with the three dials on top that you might have used when you were a kid to put your allowance in, and a few collectibles?

I'll never forget him looking up with a smile. "It just might be your lucky day," he said, as he whipped out a paper airline ticket. I didn't even know such a thing existed, but there it was, a three-layer, carbon-copy form about the size of an old manual credit card slip. He proceeded to hand-write a plane ticket on American Airlines for me to fly through London into Istanbul, narrowly getting my itinerary back on track—if all the flights were perfectly on time.

Realizing that these people might be saving my dream expedition right in front of me, I immediately switched into gratitude mode, even before I was convinced that their efforts would save the day.

The Magic of Gratitude Momentum

This is a little technique I stumbled upon that evening. As soon as you see someone making *any* effort to help you, immediately start thanking them for helping you. I have seen this build what I call *gratitude momentum*. As you continue to thank people for helping you and express your gratitude (even if they resist or respond with "now don't get your hopes up....") it builds momentum and rapport so fast, I've never had someone not help me get the outcome I wanted, or a workable alternative. Try it; you'll be stunned at how well it works if you are sincere. It is especially effective in the travel environment. Using this technique can give you a real advantage when most people are verbally attacking the gate agents. I could share a dozen other stories, but just trust me on this one.

While he came through on the ticket, he warned me. "Manley, I'm going to get you there with help from our friends over at American Airlines, but it is going to be very difficult for us to get your luggage on that plane with you. We will be working nonstop on making sure it meets you in Kyrgyzstan, though. What you need to do now is literally *run*, grab a taxi to the other terminal, and then *run* to the gate for your flight."

I don't know if you've ever been to JFK airport in New York, but let's just say it's a mess. Each terminal is like a separate airport, often requiring taxis or other ground transportation to move between, and more resilience than the average airport saga.

I thanked all three of my good-Samaritan gate agents, then took off running out the door. I hailed a cab to the next terminal and ran as fast as I could. As I approached the American Airlines gate, there was a mad, chaotic mob wrapped around the ticket counter. The gate agent was yelling at the crowd, "Go sit down if you want to get out of here tonight!"

Apparently the flight had been oversold and there were forty people standing at the gate still waiting to get on the flight. They pushed everyone back and made us all take our seats. "We said we will call you one at a time!"

At this point I presented my handwritten ticket and started into my sad little story, but the agent interrupted me: "Just sit down, sir! We will call you one at a time."

I was convinced there was no possible way I would make it on this flight, as I didn't even have an actual ticket. The people surrounding me all had real printed tickets, purchased weeks and months in advance. I began to spiral again into a slump of disappointment, exhausted and in disbelief that my trip could end right there in a JFK terminal.

They called one name after another. After about twenty-five people had been called up to the counter, they finally called my name. I ran up to the counter, grateful, thanking the gentleman. I got on the plane and searched and searched as I walked down the aisles for an open seat and my seat number. The plane was packed full, and I could not find *any* open seats, nor my seat number. Then two more amazing strokes of good fortune befell me.

Number one, I had the very last seat on the plane.

Number two, this very last seat was at a major exit point, and there was a massive open area in front of me. Leg rooms for miles. Oh yeah.

I was able to completely stretch out for the long flight from JFK to London.

We left after midnight, more than an hour behind schedule, putting me in London the next day well behind the clock and again in danger of missing a critical connection.

My pace through the London airport was slowed by additional security measures, and by the time I made it to my Turkish Air gate, the doors were sealed on the jetway and the plane was pushing off. I was almost in tears as two young Turkish Air attendants approached me and said, "We are sorry sir, the plane has left."

I told them, "I have to get to Istanbul or I will miss my flight into Kyrgyzstan. You only have two flights into Kyrgyzstan per week, so it is critical that I get into Istanbul by this evening. Please, help me. Please!"

They said, "We are sorry, sir. The plane is gone."

Now I had given up all hope and was finally able to focus on practical matters like how badly I needed to pee. I told the young Turkish Air agent, "I've got to go to the restroom. I'll be right back."

The next thing I know, I am in the restroom and I hear, "Sir, sir, sir, your flight—we have flight."

"What?" I ran out of the restroom. The Turkish Air attendants had convinced the flight, which by then had been pushed 100 yards off from the gate, to pull the plane back into the gate and unseal the door. They put me on that plane. *Seriously*. It happened.

Anything Is Possible

That entire series of events taught me an important lesson. Airlines, like all organizations, are run by people. When you get to people's hearts, people can trump policy.

What I've learned after decades of crazy travel around the world is that people can do nearly anything if they really want to. There are secret codes, a double-secret handshake, or some other mystical protocol that airlines can leverage to get you out on flights. Doors can be reopened. You name it. So the next time you find yourself in an epic scenario where you need people to help you and they resist, don't give up. Lead with gratitude, speak heart to heart, and know that anything is possible.

On a side note, when I have shared this miraculous chain of events with people, many have said, "Yeah, well, that doesn't happen post-9/11." Well, I'm here to tell you again that it *does*. In 2013, I again had a handwritten ticket bump me onto another airline, and have heard similar stories from fellow road warriors.

That long flight to Istanbul was a turning point. Not only did they bring the plane back to the gate for me, but I got an entire row all to myself to lie down and get some much-needed rest. I made it to Istanbul with plenty of time to catch the final flight into Central Asia.

During my layover in Istanbul, I engaged Turkish Air to help locate my baggage. The conclusion that I quickly came to was that it was definitely not in Istanbul, perhaps not even out of the United States yet.

Whoa.

I remember that sinking feeling as I stood at the Turkish Air desk. All my baggage was now officially lost. One small positive sliver of hope was the fact that Turkish Air stepped up and were accountable to me, their passenger. Remarkable, since they could have easily pointed the finger at my original carrier, TWA, or my transatlantic American Airlines flight. But no, they said, "We take responsibility for your baggage Mr. Feinberg. We are your airline for this trip, in partnership with these other carriers, and we will see that your baggage gets to you in Kyrgyzstan."

"When?" I asked.

"When? Oh, sir, you know this will be very difficult. We cannot say when. Perhaps soon, but not now, nor tomorrow. Maybe next week."

This was a *critical* setback. Here's how this works: No baggage, no climbing. Trip over.

So what would you do at his point? I poured on the gratitude and carried on, extremely anxious, but holding on to hope with naive optimism.

Late that evening, I flew out of Istanbul on a six-hour flight into the heart of central Asia, Bishkek, the capital city of Kyrgyzstan. Finally, after three days of nonstop travel and one last long flight, I woke up as we made our final approach.

CHAPTER 2
The First Steps into The Vertical

Have you ever had something from one area of your life inform and influence a completely different area of your life? That's how my Vertical Lessons unfolded. In my early twenties, I started to passionately pursue climbing, first in regions throughout North America, and eventually mountains around the world. My pursuit of adventure was paralleled by my love of building successful businesses. As I pursued and achieved more ambitious Vertical adventures, I became frustrated with some common challenges of being a leader in the business world that I was able to solve quite effectively in The Vertical. How was it that someone with limited resources could travel to little known regions of the world, overcome language barriers, form a team of people who had never met one another, and then unify their efforts to achieve something they weren't even sure they were capable of? After each adventure into The Vertical, I returned to my work life with a unique and inspired perspective, re-committed to helping those around me fully embrace the uncomfortable opportunities we faced together. I started to reverse engineer my Vertical experiences, and then test them in my various roles as a business leader. Some of the insights from my experiences had a profound impact on our results. I then began to share The Vertical Lessons with other organizations and discovered that they were both inspirational and impactful, providing people in nearly every industry with results they could measure in their heads and hearts.

One unexpected result from sharing The Vertical Lessons with more and more people was hearing from them many months later, that they felt both motivated and equipped to pursue crazy ideas in their lives and businesses with more courage than ever. I've learned that constant exposure to people and perspectives that help expand your vision of what's possible—ideas that at first may indeed strike you as crazy—amplify your potential in every moment of your life. That's most certainly what happened when I was introduced to The Vertical—an unforgettable turning point in my life that changed everything, one crazy idea at a time.

The first crazy idea to reach for a summit in The Vertical that was way beyond my abilities and imagination was in 1992. I was a sophomore studying psychology at Transylvania University in Lexington, Kentucky. Every weekday evening, I worked through heat, cold, sweat, and dirt for four hours loading boxes at UPS.

Beyond the incredible business lessons I learned during my three-year tenure at UPS, the friendship I developed with my supervisor, Mark Williams, changed the trajectory of my life forever. Mark is a positive force of nature. His boundless energy, irresistible enthusiasm for everything, and beautiful heart make for the kind of friend we all need more of. I respected Mark, trusted him, and was inspired to engage in any idea he uttered. So when Mark said "Manley, you really need to come check out the wilderness of the Red River Gorge with me," I couldn't wait.

The Red River Gorge, in eastern Kentucky, is a truly mind-blowing and special place. Once unknown, it is no longer a secret, enjoyed by thousands of climbers from around the world every year. After adventures to more than 400 climbing areas on the planet, I can now say Mark and the early pioneers of the area were absolutely right; the Red River is world-class. Mark encouraged me to take my first step into The Vertical of the Red River Gorge early that spring. That first step launched me into a new world of adventure. Little did I know it would change me forever.

What stands out the most about my first weekend on the rock with Mark was how present I instantly became when I stepped up onto a ten-foot boulder. The challenge was intense and immediate, and the reward of sitting on top after struggling to find my way resonated well beyond my conscious thoughts, *connecting* deep within my soul. I felt like I was plugged into a massive source of energy and joy, and I wanted more. More, of course, meant to climb higher, through more struggle, onto an even more rewarding summit. I remember Mark being impressed with my ability to claw to the top of the small boulders that weekend. It was not for any athletic ability, as I believe it was the first time in my life that I had shown above-average aptitude for any physical pursuit. I do believe it was that connection to something bigger inside me, to something *infinitely* bigger out there, that engaged me so powerfully. Fully energized by the experience, I enthusiastically said to Mark, "I gotta climb higher!"

"Well, you'll need a rope and gear, and you'll have to learn the systems to protect yourself, Manley."

The next stop was Phillip Gall's, an outdoor adventure outfitter in Lexington, Kentucky. Like a kid walking into a toy store for the first time, I explored the wares with wonder. Then I met Tim behind the climbing gear counter. Sharing my newfound passion for The

Vertical with him, I asked, "What do I need to get started?" He recommended a dynamic climbing rope (one that will stretch when you fall to reduce impact) and a nylon harness to attach the rope to my body when I climbed. "You'll need three more key items for now," he said, laying a few feet of nylon webbing, four carabiners, and a figure-8 on the counter. He explained that the webbing was round-woven seatbelt-like material to tie around trees and suspend the rope from. He then described how the lightweight aluminum carabiners were clasps to connect the rope to the webbing, and that the figure-8 would allow me to descend the rope as well as lock the rope off to stop another climber's fall. Finally, he most enthusiastically encouraged me to buy climbing shoes—goofy, bright green high-tops that had special black sticky rubber soles to grip the rock. I resisted his suggestion, explaining "my old combat boots seem to be working just fine." Without hesitation, and with sincere and savvy skill, he clearly articulated, "I can tell you are serious about climbing. These aren't required, but are essential if you want to climb high. You won't believe how much difference they make. Compared to your boots or tennis shoes, these will help you make much harder moves. You'll have way more fun with these on your feet. Trust me."

Trust me.

This was the first of many times in my journey to learn how to safely explore The Vertical that I would need to trust someone. Even though I had never seen this man climb, I accepted him as competent, because he delivered his counter-side advice with great confidence.

I asked him, "What is this going to cost me?" I almost fell over when he totaled it up.

"Three hundred bucks and some change." Here I was, in

college, with no money. As I left the store, in a moment my passion trumped my patience. I decided to do the only thing a kid could do. I called my Mom.

I stepped out of the store and paced nervously in a small circle as I called her from a pay phone nearby. For a second time in a few weeks, I again shared my passion for climbing with my Mom, telling her about my second visit to the Red River Gorge with Mark and friends the previous weekend. "Oh, Lord son! Well, I can tell you are on fire with this new climbing thing, and I know I'm not going to talk you out of it. What do you need to be safe?"

"I'm so glad you asked Mom. I need 300 dollars."

"I want you to get what you need to be safe, son."

That day she went beyond her comfort zone, both financially and as a parent. She made a wise choice to equip me with what I needed to safely explore this new chapter of my life. Like any good parent (or leader), my Mom recognized the embers of a passion in me, then did everything in her power to help me pursue it and grow the fire within.

Light the Fire First

First came the drive and desire; then I learned how I could explore more and do it safely.

Me and my mom, Pat, Christmas, 1999

Within six months, I met a new friend, climber Travis Moore. I'll never forget where we were standing in the newly opened Climb Time climbing gym in Lexington, Kentucky, when he looked at me and said, "Manley, did you know there are walls so big that you can climb all day and still not make it to the top? You have to sleep on the side of the walls for days before you ever even reach the summit!"

"What? No way!"

"Yeah. El Capitan in Yosemite, California, for example. Can you imagine how amazing that would be? Yeah, man, they call it big wall climbing."

El Capitan, Yosemite National Park, California: Photo by Josh Hawkins

I didn't just imagine; I started dreaming.

The more I learned, the more intrigued I became. Then my intrigue grew into an obsession. A deep, burning desire to live out the experience. My drive to climb El Capitan was never about reaching the summit, but the deep immersion in the journey and experience of living on a wall.

That's what I've always enjoyed most when climbing; how it feels to *embrace the exposure* of being outside of our comfort zone. The presence it demands. The deep, intense bond that is formed when you join forces with another human, connecting your lives together by tying your climbing rope to each other. Holding that rope as you step up into the unknown, your lives literally in each other's hands. The grind and frustration of the struggle, the joy and euphoria of achievement.

That's why I believe it is *worth it*. I hope that having a sense of what is possible in your life inspires you to *Step Up into The Vertical* with me.

Throughout this book, I invite you to consider and reflect on The Vertical Perspective you gain along the way. At the end of each of chapter, I'll encourage you to take action and offer strategic and tactical frameworks I've developed to help you start applying the lessons and build *Vertical Momentum* in your life today.

This may sound simple, but this is a big ask. Aren't you busy enough already? I encourage you to ask yourself, *is it worth it?* After more than twenty years of applying The Vertical Lessons in a wide range of business and personal scenarios, I've seen results in myself and others that are both tangible and beyond quantification. Seeing a team member show up more engaged, then stand out to earn the respect and recognition of their organization. Then seeing them be promoted, making more money so they can support their family and forge a better life. Weathering challenging economics. The joy of seeing the top and bottom line of your business grow.

Perhaps most rewarding of all: imagine walking into your home more fulfilled than frustrated, with more of your best left over for those who love and need you most. That is worth it.

SECTION TWO
The Vertical Lessons

CHAPTER 3

Vertical Lesson 1:
Decide If It's Worth It

I couldn't believe my eyes when I saw the meager landing strip in Bishkek, Kyrgyzstan, and its bizarre airport.

Walking off the plane and into the baggage claim area was shocking. Imagine stepping into a bare, unpainted cinderblock building with a single light bulb swinging from a ragged electric wire in the center of a dimly lit square room. The floor was filthy. A U-shaped set of rollers allowed the luggage to be shuffled around the room as my fellow passengers happily retrieved their bags. I watched the baggage come through and around, still holding on to the possibility that my gear could be with me.

No bags.

The only good news was that my brother was there to pick me up. A huge hug and a brief moment of joy was had, then his massive smile quickly vanished as he looked around and said, "Bro! Where's your gear? Oh no; we may be completely screwed, that sucks! It's going to be really hard to get your baggage back. We've got about three days to get your bags and our supplies together to stay on our schedule, or your expedition is over."

I had allowed five weeks for the entire expedition, including travel time. I know this may sound like an eternity, but it was just barely enough time for all the logistics involved. Between the flights and the effort it would take to get into the remote valleys of Kyrgyzstan, we had very little wiggle room for any more logistical setbacks. We immediately went to work trying to get the baggage located. Ultimately, what saved me was my Turkish friend in the United States, Hasaan Altindag. He put his Turkish language skills to work for my cause, calling Turkish Air offices around the world at all hours of the night and day, pleading with them to help me locate my bags. Finally, on the last possible day, we went to the Turkish Air office in Bishkek and found all three of my wayward bags, remarkably intact.

Bishkek in itself was an amazing experience, as soon as I was able to see the beautiful culture beneath the surface of the sprawl. Feeling quite desperate at first glance, the concrete shell of an existence was once a thriving city at the height of the former Soviet Republic. Bishkek once served as a crossroads in central Asia, an intriguing blend of Russian, Mongolian, Kyrgyz, and Islamic cultures. During the Cold War, the city served as a primary base for the Soviet-supported climbing community. The Soviet Republic valued mountain climbers highly and fully supported them so they could focus on training and conquering the world's peaks to proudly plant the Soviet flag and spread the illusion of Soviet dominance in the world. Similar to being an Olympic athlete, being a climber in the Soviet Union was a huge honor; a rare place and time when climbers were treated as national heroes. As I traveled through the region, I learned that when a local perceived me as an *alpinisto*, the locals' name for mountain climbers, it called back to the glory days of the Soviet Union and somehow granted me a more forgiving and pleasant encounter, especially during my interactions with local "authorities."

Three Kyrgyz men hanging out in Bishkek, Kyrgyzstan

We were in limbo as we waited for our bags. Not knowing whether the expedition was going to happen, we kept postponing buying the proper supplies, including most critically, food. Then, when my bags did show up, we were pleasantly surprised and caught off guard. We had to hastily speed up our exit from the city before we were fully equipped. We planned to address this issue later, with the assumption that we could simply fuel up with proper expedition and food supplies in the small town of Batkin, the last outpost on the way to the Aksu Valley. This strategy proved to be a critical mistake.

The next morning, we went to the Bishkek market. We struggled to find a driver willing to make the journey to the mountains, for a reasonable rate, with a vehicle that could hold us and our gear. We eventually compromised. The first issue we had to

Mother and child in Bishkek, Kyrgyzstan

Craig assessing the dismal supplies at the local mountain equipment shop in Bishkek

be willing to deal with was that the driver only had a UAZ (a Soviet military version of a Jeep) that seated six. This may sound adequate, but we were transporting my brother and me, the driver and his daughter whom he insisted come along, and Misha, a young local whom I had hired to guard my tent and gear in base camp.

A major problem was we had almost no room for our gear. This pushed us to have bags at our feet, between us, and beside us, with not a single extra inch of room to breathe. Not a big deal if you are making a twenty-minute drive, but we were looking at twenty-four to forty-eight hours of nonstop Third-World mountain road misery. The second challenge was that our driver had only agreed to take us to Batken. We would have to repeat our search for the next driver in a much, much smaller town. Bummer.

We were faced with the same question that comes up in most any business or life endeavor when an obstacle appears.

Two Kyrgyz men, obviously suspicious of the Westerner with the camera

Were we willing to continue despite this setback? This question is a reasonable one, but if it's the only one you ask, you may find yourself giving up too soon. The challenge I have with this specific question is that it focuses on the obstacles and the trial immediately ahead without refocusing on the ultimate summit you are pursuing. There's a better question to ask first. Is the summit worth it? Refocusing on the summit first, and using the question in that broader, zoomed-out context will often help rebalance perspective, reduce the emotional gravity of imminent setbacks, and help us make a better choice. When we contemplated the bigger goal, the answer to the secondary question—*are we willing to continue despite this setback?*—was easy to answer. Yes!

The lack of room in the vehicle and a commitment to only take us two-thirds of the way was not the worst part. It turns out

Buying a few basic supplies the old-school way in Bishkek

these particular UAZs do not have big fuel tanks, and the mountain roads on our intended journey did not have adequate gas stations.

This may be hard to believe for a first-world reader, but imagine a country so remote and wild that the only way you can make a long journey is to either bring all the gas you need with you, or piece together the necessary fuel by stopping to buy any gas you can, at every opportunity, even when the amount available seems ridiculous. Finding enough gas to make the trip to Batken was a serious concern hanging over our head. On three occasions, we stopped to buy a few Coca-Cola bottles of fuel from a youngster selling it on the side of the road. At other lucky moments, just in time, we were able to replenish our tank and the one backup tank that was strapped to the outside of the UAZ.

After more than a day of epic travel, we finally arrived in the town of Batken, Kyrgyzstan. With a population of around 10,000,

Dude + bottle of gas + road = central Asian gas station

we expected to be able to stock up on food supplies, but we were shocked when our UAZ driver dropped us off at the Batken market. It consisted of a few rows of folding tables baking in the sun with meager food offerings. It must have been a bumper crop year for potatoes in a nearby region, as that was about all you could buy. So that's what we bought—a lot more potatoes, more ramen noodles, and a bottle of Thai garlic chili paste. Even in this last effort to stock up with enough food, we grossly underestimated our potato needs, and even more critically, our ability to *eat* potatoes for twenty days straight.

Women contemplating life at the Batken market

Our next task was to find a ride from Batken to Vorukh, Tajikistan, the final stopping point before our trek on foot into the mountains of central Asia. Craig and Misha found a taxi driver who was willing to drive us to Tajikistan, but he only had a compact

Happy and vibrant at the Batken market

Three women catching up at the Batken market

car for the journey; a classic Lada sedan. The Russian-made Lada was apparently *the* car to drive in central Asia, jamming nearly every street we traveled. If we thought the UAZ ride had been tight, this leg of the trip would set a new level of discomfort and quite possibly a record for volume of gear and humans that could be stuffed into a little Lada. Four grown men, about ten large duffels of equipment and pounds of potatoes packed into a crumbling compact jalopy. Miserable.

Off we went over mountain passes for another day of arduous travel. Through dirt and debris, we rolled through the mountains and finally arrived in the small village of Vorukh, Tajikistan, on July 8th.

In 1924, Joseph Stalin sliced up and redefined borders throughout central Asia to dilute the ethnic populations of the Russian empire. Stalin believed that by erratically drawing boarders and creating small countries within other countries, he could minimize the chance of a revolution by any specific ethnic group. The result of his effort remains a convoluted and very difficult border system where you can be traveling in one country, Kyrgyzstan as an example, and then have to pass into Tajikistan or Uzbekistan, and then back into Kyrgyzstan within an hour or two.

This would be similar to driving through your town, and when you go into the next area of town, you actually cross an international border into a completely different country. Then, after some more driving, you exit that country and you are now back in your original country. Now keep driving, and then you again cross another border, which is actually *a third* country.

It is quite bizarre and would otherwise be a nonissue if it weren't for completely corrupt border guards who leap at every chance to extort cash from travelers.

By law, you're not supposed to need a visa to travel through these "in-holdings," but that doesn't stop any of the desperate so-called police or border patrol officials from trying to steal your money (or put you in prison for a few months). Fortunately, my brother was well adept at negotiating, which usually required Craig getting in people's faces, screaming, and challenging their corruption. A global business nomad of many, many years, he is the most knowledgeable and experienced world traveler I've ever met. Time and time again, he directly confronted corrupt officer after corrupt officer and refused payment. Most of the time, they backed down. In only two cases did we make a small "donation" to allow us to get on with our journey.

The fact that we had a Kyrgyzstan visa as required, and none for Uzbekistan and Tajikistan irritated the border guards and gave them another excuse to extort money from us. This constant harassment put all of us on edge; we knew that simply meeting the wrong authority anywhere along the road could end our expedition and land us in a local jail.

The journey from Batken to Vorukh seemed to take forever, but the anxiety provoked by what I learned next made our final stopping point come all too fast. Misha, our base camp guard, started describing in broken English that there had been some problems in Vorukh, Tajikistan, the previous year. "Manfree, last year in Vorukh there was problem. Last year was machine-gun" *(sounds of machine gun from Misha)* "was problem, hostages, bang bang machine gun, problem. This year, maybe no problem, maybe problem. Last year was problem, but then was no problem."

"What?" My heart rate made my head start to spin as I instantly got sick to my stomach.

"I said problem, no problem; what are you worried about, Manfree?"

"Did you say maybe machine guns?"

"Manfree, maybe problem, no problem. Don't worry, probably no problem."

Problem, no problem. Misha used this phrase in every other sentence so much that we ended up nicknaming him "no problem." At this point, a haunting phrase of fear slipped into my head: "You are going to die on this trip." I was scared. And I should have been.

While Misha's mispronunciation of my name as "Manfree" had become endearing, his ambiguous "problem, no problem" wasn't the detail I needed to ease my mind. After returning to American soil, I discovered that the areas where we had been traveling— specifically Vorukh, Tajikistan, the Uzbekistan border, and the Kyrgyzstan border where we were to start our journey on foot—were actually crossroads and a hotbed of terrorism. Multiple cells of terrorists had been active in the region, along with extraordinary tension and violence injected by the Islamic Movement of Uzbekistan, or IMU. With direct allegiance and connection to al-Qaeda and the Taliban, the IMU had launched raids into this region through 1999 and 2000, setting the stage for our expedition to turn into a disaster at literally any turn in the road ahead.

We arrived in Vorukh late in the afternoon and were surprised to find teenage AK-47–wielding border guards quite welcoming. There were no hotels, grocery stores, or typical infrastructure. Laced between dusty streets and a river passing by the edge of the impoverished settlement were a number of homes in the remote Third-World village. My brother immediately went to work negotiating for a place for us to stay. The "sheriff" of the village said he could provide shelter for us, donkeys and men to help us make the multiday trek to our destination the following morning.

The sheriff, his family, and his cohorts were very friendly. It seemed that we had lucked out and were protected by the chance of connecting with him when we had arrived that afternoon. His family got to work making dinner, and as the sun set on the mysterious mountains just beyond town, our meal was served. We were treated to *plov*, the national dish of Tajikistan. The mix of rice, carrots, and mutton was rather greasy and put my stomach to the test. Craig said we should be happy we weren't being served horsemeat, which is also popular in central Asia. I choked down as much as I could eat, because I needed nourishment and I really did not want to upset the sheriff. Aside from the stomach-turning nature of the food, I found the endless cups of tea, along with other local offerings of cucumber, fruit, and bread with the colorful locals to be mesmerizing. We sat with our legs crossed on

Craig negotiating room, board, and donkeys in Vorukh, Tajikistan

A beautiful group of children in Vorukh

their back porch around a beautiful handmade Tajik rug eating with shared utensils and shared plates. The experience was surreal and felt almost like an out-of-body experience. I became intensely aware of how strange and exotic every second was, deeply embedded in the unspoiled culture of that wild place while time seemed to stand still.

I knew right then and there that it was an extraordinary once-in-a-lifetime experience, and I was giddy with joy, truly able to finally enjoy the trip for perhaps the first time. I was present. I was exhausted, yet excited; our trek would begin in the quickly-approaching early hours of the following morning.

Dinner with the sheriff of Vorukh, Misha (aka "No Problem"), me, Craig and one of our Tajik donkey guides

As the evening grew later, vodka emerged, along with local Tajiks and Russians, who stumbled by and joined our back-porch party at the sheriff's house. The next morning came way too soon. Being hung over in Tajikistan, central Asia was exceptionally painful. Any other day, any other place, and I might have slept it off, but my dream of the massive granite walls of the valleys motivated me to get on with it.

Before dawn, we loaded up donkeys and started our trek towards the Aksu Valley. One full day of hiking brought us to the remains of a small stone home. The floor was dirt, but the structure was solid and provided just enough shelter inside and helped us save time by not having to set up tents. The next morning, we pushed hard to finish the approach into the Aksu Valley. Walking through narrow canyons and underneath massive walls of unstable rock, we trudged on for hours.

Inside an abandoned small stone home with our two Tajik donkey guides

I'll never forget walking through the valley that morning and finding a very old man sitting on a rock. With no other people nor

Craig, Misha, Tajik man, and donkey taking shelter during our trek into the Aksu Valley

any place to live anywhere in sight, his sudden appearance felt like the Twilight zone, as though I had hallucinated him sitting there. He appeared to be an ancient nomad, as if he had walked straight out of the Old Testament, and had been sitting on his rock since Jesus had walked by. He just stared back at us as we trekked by and said "hello." I bet you he is still sitting there right now.

Finally, late on the evening of July 10, after grinding away on the trail all day, we made a turn near the Karavishin River, and Misha smiled as he announced, "Soon, Manley, no problem, the Aksu Valley. Problem, no problem. Tonight sleep below mountains; no problem, no machine gun." Now *that* certainty made me smile.

Barely beating the sunset, we made the final grind up the valley as the incredible Aksu Valley revealed itself to our weary eyes. As we hiked around a final bend in the trail, we saw my brother's friend, Josh Denys, who had made the trek into the valley

Ancient man sitting on a rock since Jesus walked by. I'm willing to bet he's still sitting there.

A first view of three of the many amazing walls in the Aksu Valley

ahead of our arrival. He was an aid worker my brother had met who had some solid climbing experience. I felt relieved to at least have a partner for a few days, but knowing both Josh and Craig's available time to stay in the valley was limited, we got to work quickly. We unpacked our gear and set up our tents in a most surreal spot, right below The Russian Tower of granite, a few hundred feet from the roaring river. This massive Russian Tower is one of the most infamous formations in the region. It had been a very specific part of my dream as it was a featured summit of success from the 1995 North Face expedition to the valley. Its sheer granite and symmetric face stood out in a hall of giants. Surrounding us were wildflowers, the occasional wild mountain oxen and the hypnotic flow of the river. After agreeing on a pickup date with our porters, we said goodbye to them and their team of donkeys as the last rays of light chased the horizon.

Nomadic Kyrgyz family in the Aksu Valley

As we unpacked our supplies, we realized that we were set as far as mountain equipment, but desperately short of food. Our strike-out in the Batkin market would gradually affect our enjoyment of our final dream destination more and more each day. I mean, you get *hungry* in the mountains, and the first few days, anything tastes amazing. But one can only get so excited about living on ramen noodles, potatoes, and oatmeal, day in and day out. The only key staple we'd bought enough of was tea. It was a case of Earl Grey. One problem; I love a little sugar in my tea. And we didn't bring any. (You would think this would be no big deal, and that I might make the most of a great opportunity to learn to enjoy tea in a healthier way—sugar-free. This little joyful culinary detail became magnified to represent the "we *almost* have a heavenly setup here" reality of our spartan base camp.)

For our first full day in the Aksu Valley, we rested and enjoyed some glorious weather. This was short-lived. The day after we arrived, a funky rain system set in, driving us into our small backpacking tents, where we struggled to find enough room to sit up, eat, and live without cramping our backs and necks. We spent most of our waking hours for the next three days holed up in our tents, just hoping the weather would clear to give us an opportunity to climb. There was only one other party in the Aksu Valley at the time, an Italian team who had obviously been to this Third-World expedition rodeo before. They were very well prepared, complete with an Uzbek mountain guide named Andre to help them with logistics. Andre had been a Soviet *alpinisto* star, summiting Everest with no oxygen, and had completed ascents of most major walls in the region. In addition to Andre, the Italian team also had a couple who served as base camp managers, primarily focusing on ensuring the three Italian mountain

Craig at our base camp below the Russian Tower

Three stately young nomads in the Aksu Valley

guides had plenty of food to eat all day and night when they weren't
in The Vertical, forging a first ascent. A first ascent is when a new
route is climbed where none previously existed. Fortunately for us,
the Italian team and their supporting base camp crew were very
friendly and seemed to feel some empathy for our pitifully equipped
operation. Their first neighborly gesture was to give us a box of sugar
cubes. Oh, the joy in such simple gifts! Josh and I spent some time
talking with Andre to get his opinion about what routes might be
good options for us to attempt.

Andre told us of a 2,400-foot wall in the neighboring Kara-Su
Valley called the Yellow Wall. Cloaked heavily in his Russian accent,
his description of the "diagonal route" immediately captivated our
attention and inspired us to spin up our engines of desire. The
number one reason we got excited about the diagonal wall was that
Andre believed it was relatively easy compared to all the routes
in both valleys, and he claimed it was just a two-hour hike to the

base. He estimated that we could summit in one very long day, and perhaps only need to endure one night of suffering out in the exposed environment before we returned back to base camp. This route, like many in the alpine world, presented a dilemma: take no camping gear and minimal supplies so you can move fast, in hopes of a one-day ascent, or, at least double (if not triple) the weight and bulk of your supplies and plan for living on the wall for more than a day, knowing the extra weight and complications of dealing with extra gear will dramatically slow your ascent. Either way, you are going to pay a price for the summit.

After two hours of deliberation, we decided to go light and attempt to make the approach, climb and summit, descend to the base, *and* trek back to our base camp in only one day. Looking back, it surely was an ambitious plan.

We packed up our gear and left early the next morning under mixed skies, hoping the angry clouds would lose their daily battle with the sun. Andre's "easy two-hour walk" ended up being over five hours of strenuous hiking, a physical grind over a mountain pass, and down into the Kara-Su valley to the south. By the time we got to the base of the Yellow Wall the morning had slipped away, not at all what we intended.

Having brought no gear to sleep on the wall and no food for dinner, we had just enough water and snacks to make a fast ascent. We knew the odds were stacked against us when we roped up at the base, but we thought we should give it a shot. Certainly if we didn't at least try, our chances for success were zero. Just after noon, we started gunning up the route.

Josh Denys coiling rope for our attempt on the Yellow Wall in the Kara-Su Valley

The Yellow Wall, Kara Su Valley, Kyrgyzstan

Roping Up and Pitches

Roping up is a final step you take on the ground before stepping into The Vertical. It is the moment when each person ties one end of the rope into their nylon harness to connect to their partner, establishing a lifeline between them. The typical lifeline is fifty or sixty meters (165 to 200 feet) long, giving the team up to 200 feet of rope to break the climb into sections, which are known as *pitches* of climbing.

Climbing is a complete test of mind and body. From the safety of terra firma, you step up onto the wall, reaching with your hands to grab onto the biggest protrusion or opening in the wall you can find, followed by placing the edge of your climbing shoe on something at about knee high so you can step up and reach higher. Sometimes the best option for your fingers to cling to, or your foot to rest on, might be as small as the edge of knife. On easier routes you might find larger features, or *holds,* to pull on. With your hands clasping onto holds above, and your feet pasted onto something near your knees, you step up against the force of gravity pulling you down and reach higher to find the next hold for your hands.

Think of it as climbing a tree, but instead of nice, round branches to grab, you are often forced to grasp very small features on the wall, requiring an equal supply of grip strength and desire. As you repeat the process, your body is often pushed to its flexibility limits as you stretch. It also requires great core strength on more difficult moves as you try to stabilize and balance while you push with your legs and hang on with your hands. Before long, muscular fatigue starts flooding your mind with doubt and fear. This usually happens about the same time your mind starts to fear falling, amplifying the physical challenge. The fear and physical demands often start feeding a vicious downward spiral of resistance, sometimes paralyzing you on the wall. Developing mental focus and the ability to manage fear is as critical as physical strength and endurance. "Can I really trust my foot on this little edge of rock? Will my forearm keep my fingers wrapped around that tiny hold as I pull myself up?" As in life, your internal dialog constantly tests your courage and confidence.

The type of holds you have to choose varies greatly depending on the type of rock you are climbing. In the remote mountain valleys in Kyrgyzstan, and most major mountain ranges, exposed rock is typically granite. Granite is often hard and solid enough to trust your hands and feet to, but it typically yields very few holds for you to simply grab or step up on. The fastest way to the top of large granite walls is to follow cracks in the granite. Climbing cracks requires a unique set of skills. It demands mastery of subtle techniques with your fingers, hands, and fists, as well as methods for wedging anything from your toe to your entire leg into the crack, depending on the width of the crack you are facing. To most people, climbing up a blank wall using only cracks to place your hands and feet feels quite insecure and is also painful, unless you've spent years climbing on similar rock to hone your crack-climbing techniques. While I had clocked many days on mountain granite in areas like Yosemite National Park in California, it was not my comfort zone. I had been raised climbing on the forgiving sandstone walls of the southeastern United States, where the faces are typically well featured, with generous-sized holds to grab and place your feet on. This difference created one more element of discomfort in Kyrgyzstan.

On the bright side, cracks in the granite walls provide a way to protect yourself against a fall. One person is designated as the leader, climbing up the wall while the other person is responsible for holding their rope. As the leader moves up, he or she looks for places in the cracks of the wall to place climbing gear and clip the rope into the rock to stop a potential fall. Ideally, the leader finds openings in the wall that are just the right size for the gear on hand at the time. A team will usually take between fifteen and twenty-five pieces of lead-climbing gear, ranging in size from 1/8" to 3.5" wide. The lead climber must carefully manage the selection of gear as a crucial resource. While it could essentially eliminate any concern of falling any real distance, gear also can't be placed constantly during the climb. If it were, the leader would run out of gear before finishing the climbing pitch. This requires the leader on each pitch to try and anticipate the difficulty of the climbing ahead as well as what size gear might be needed to protect against a fall. In a difficult section, the lead climber might place a piece of gear every twelve feet or so, exposing him or her to a fall of up to twenty-four feet should a slip occur before the next piece is placed. When the climbing ahead looks easier, the leader will often "run it out," climbing twenty or more feet before placing a piece of gear to ensure a decent selection of equipment to build an *anchor* at the end of the pitch of climbing. The leader builds an anchor either because he or she has run out of rope or has found a good place to rest, such as a feature or small ledge where the team will be able to stand and recover before the next section of climbing.

Anchor

Built from three or more redundant pieces gear; it provides a solid and absolutely trustworthy connection for the party to the wall.

As soon as Josh and I launched into The Vertical at Aksu, we immediately struggled with some physically difficult sections, getting lost in the maze of crack systems running in every direction. It is easy to get lost on a rock wall, especially when you do not have a good map to guide you and help you navigate past features you can identify, such as a ledge or roof, corners or prominent crack systems. All we had to guide us was our memory of Andre's vague description of the route, so it felt as though we were on a first ascent. Finding the easiest path up became our biggest challenge, but after a few hundred feet of wandering back and forth as we climbed up a buttress, we found a series of cracks that provided a more obvious passage. This helped us settle into a cadence and gain some confidence, enabling us to knock out about 600 feet of climbing in just a few hours. Just as we started building momentum, a storm front was doing the same.

What had started as an overcast morning developed into an ugly afternoon as we tried to optimistically ignore the nasty-looking storm system grinding its way over the northwest ridge of the surrounding peaks behind us. The promise of knocking out more than 700 feet of climbing in a few hours was drowned out by the sickening, stomach-churning feeling of knowing we were about to be in a serious situation—completely exposed, with no shelter, on a sheer, remote granite face.

With no shelter gear, one energy bar each, and less than a liter of water left, we were forced to contemplate the mountain's most intimidating factor. We were pretty sure the climbing ahead was significantly more difficult than what we had covered so far. Add in the weather bearing down on us, and we had multiple factors in our face that we couldn't ignore. It wasn't about comfort. We were fully committed to enduring misery as needed, but putting ourselves in a life-threatening situation was not an option we could consciously choose. You would think this would be an easy decision.

Here are a few reasons why retreat from a major objective is never as straightforward as you might think. First, we really wanted to summit. We were committed, inspired, and ready to be *uncomfortable,* because we knew it would be *worth it.* Second, retreat can offer more challenges and danger than continuing on. And finally, from a tactical standpoint, we really didn't have the ideal equipment to improvise a new descent route down the face of the mountain.

On some climbs, you are able to descend the route the same way you climbed up, using permanent anchors people have established, making retreat a relatively straightforward affair. Permanent anchors can include something as secure as a metal ring attached to the wall with an incredibly strong construction bolt (referred to as bolted anchors), or strong nylon material safely tied to trees or features on the wall you can thread your rope through, descend, and then pull your rope down. Due to the remote and adventurous nature of the walls in Kyrgyzstan, they see very little climbing traffic, and there are very few permanent anchors. Our route had none.

Ideally, in this scenario, you would be able to create your own bolted anchors on the way down if needed, giving you a very comfortable margin of safety, but we did not have the equipment to establish bolted anchors. We had counted on reaching the summit and descending via the previously established descent route, and had not brought extra gear to leave behind on a new descent route. Nobody likes leaving climbing equipment behind; it is fairly expensive, $25-$75 per piece of gear you leave. Obviously that's a small price to pay for safety, but if you leave too many pieces behind, you can run out of gear and strand yourself on the mountain. Or perhaps you get down safely, but leave so much equipment behind that you eliminate any other chance you may have had to climb for the rest of the expedition.

We weighed all the information we had and decided we had to descend at once. With all the concern around leaving some of our gear behind as we made our emergency descent, we carefully started rappelling down the face in search of trees or other natural features in the rock that we could tie nylon rope to and create safe and inexpensive anchors.

 Rappelling is a mechanical method of sliding down the rope with a device that allows you to vary the friction between the rope and device to control your rate of descent. While rappelling can often be a person's first exposure to navigating the gravity of The Vertical, experienced climbers know it can be the most dangerous part of climbing. Relying on a single anchor system, coupled with exhaustion and the complicated logistics of descending is the reason more climbers are killed getting down a mountain than climbing up.

Our decision was timely. We were able to start rappelling before the rain hit and safely descended the 700 feet to the base of the Yellow Wall, only having to leave behind one piece of climbing gear and a few pieces of inexpensive nylon rope as we retreated to the safety of the ground below.

We were completely exhausted at this point and out of food. We had grossly underestimated our calorie consumption needs and we were also out of water, but we had iodine tablets to purify any water we could collect once we got down to the river below. We hiked down, got some water in our bottles and excavated some electrolyte packets from the bottoms of our packs, giving us just enough fuel to get moving on our long trek back to our base camp in the other valley.

As we ascended the mountain pass, the last dim, overcast light of day vanished and a heavy fog set in. Wild yaks were meandering through the fog, creating a very strange, dreamlike experience. That's when we really slammed into the physical wall of exhaustion.

Stumbling along, lost in the fog of the mountain pass, I said, "Josh, let's just rest for a moment. I am worked!" Josh didn't reply with words, but in full agreement, collapsed beside me. Our intention was to just catch our breath, but before we knew it, we slipped into a weird, half-sleep, dream state, completely disconnected from time, barely connected with our space on the mountain pass. We don't know how long we were there sleeping. We estimate that it was one to two hours before Josh shook me. "Manley! We gotta get moving. Come on, man!" We resumed our march, staggering through the fog and down the maze of mountain paths. Finally, we found our way back to and across our river in the Aksu Valley.

Those last few hours are gone from my memory, but I will always remember the relief I felt when we saw our tents as we rounded the bend in the valley. Finally, at 2:30 a.m., we crawled into our sleeping bags and collapsed.

That was my one chance to climb with an English-speaking American partner, as Josh had to head back to work the day after. This experience was definitely positive, in that I got a sense of how difficult the rock climbing was going to be, and it enabled me to get in some training and acclimatizing while trying to figure out what I would do next.

Like losing any good team member, Josh's exit was a clear setback to my momentum. He was very competent in The Vertical, making the goodbye even more disheartening.

That wasn't the worst of it. Not only was Josh going back; within a few more days, my brother Craig had to leave as well.

I thought the decision Josh and I had faced on the Yellow Wall was difficult, but it was just the beginning. The next three uncomfortable decisions would prove to be most fateful.

The first of the decisions was pretty straightforward; would I give up on my dream climb and head back with Craig? Or stay in the remote valley? Would it be *worth it?*

Vertical Momentum: From Insight to Action

It was June 9th, 2015, in Denver, Colorado. After a two-day meeting as part of a strategic advisory board for an association, I sat down with my friend Vance Brown, co-founder and CEO of Cherwell Software, who was also attending. In the sunshine of the Colorado mountains, we started working on ideas regarding how we could make our keynotes for his upcoming global user conference as meaningful and valuable as possible for everyone in attendance. I had presented my signature keynote for their conference the previous year, and after getting to know Vance and how simpatico our hearts and minds were, we felt we had an opportunity to completely build something from the ground up that would take our efforts to another level. Our high-level plan was for Vance to do the opening conference keynote and for me to do the closing keynote, calling back to and reinforcing his messages.

Within minutes of sitting down, Vance enthusiastically shared a theme he had been considering. "I got to see Ron Howard speak, Manley; it was incredible. He was finishing up work producing and directing his new movie, *In the Heart of the Sea*, a true story of epic survival based on the sinking of the whaling ship *Essex*, which became the inspiration for the epic novel, *Moby-Dick*. After his presentation, during a Q&A session, an attendee asked a pointed question. 'Mr. Howard, how do you get Hollywood stars to endure such grueling conditions? How do you make them *comfortable*?' His response was brilliant. 'My job is not to make it *comfortable*; my job is to make it *worth it*.' Isn't that powerful Manley?"

"Yes! I wish I had said that, Vance!"

"So that's what I'm thinking of for our theme—*uncomfortable, but worth it*."

It was perfect! Completely aligning with my core message and Vance's message for his customers and his company, we rolled up our sleeves and started working to develop our keynote programs. Like anything worthwhile, we both endured many uncomfortable moments to create our vision of what we thought was possible. We both explored experiences and lessons from our past that were painfully uncomfortable to share with our audience. They would require us to show up, more vulnerable and transparent than ever, exposing some of our darkest moments and our struggles to become better humans every day. There were several points along the way that summer where we each considered giving up on what we had envisioned. We knew it would be much easier to fall back on safer material and insights that we were comfortable sharing, but we couldn't stop climbing, because we had a sense of what was possible. We believed that what we were developing could be very powerful and serve our audience in a deep and meaningful way. We *knew* that it would be *worth it*.

At those most difficult inflection points, when the resistance of gravity had increased to a level in our hearts and minds that we nearly abandoned our plans, we asked a powerful question. It was the same question I had asked myself when I faced the many tests and trials of my journey in Kyrgyzstan. *Is it worth it?*

Vance Brown and I exploring uncomfortable personal territory in the mountains above Bear Trap Ranch, Colorado Springs Colorado, August 17, 2015

The question is a powerful one, helping us transcend the pain of the moment to refocus on *why* we were committed.

Sometimes a simple reminder of what the end result will be can give us the clarity and reignite our drive to persevere. In the most trying moment, you may need to go deeper before you can climb higher. The following questions will help you reexamine, reconsider, and recommit to your efforts, ultimately helping you *decide if it's worth it.* Contemplating this exercise in your mind can be effective, but be ready to write when you're really feeling the dreadful funk of gravity in your mind.

Is It Worth It?

My next summit is:

_____

When I reach the summit, I imagine the following view, feeling, and new perspective:

_____

_____

Reaching my next summit will serve the following people:

_____

_____

Imagine an encounter in the future with someone your courageous effort helps. What do they say to you when they thank you and share how you've helped them with your efforts?

_____

_____

From my next summit, I will probably be able to see the following possibilities and next summits:

_____

_____

My next summit will be worth it because:

_____

_____

CHAPTER 4

Vertical Lesson 2: Declare Your Current Climb

Have you ever had a moment in your life when an opportunity came your way, and you went for it? Then, one day, you wake up and ask yourself, "What have I gotten myself into?" That's *exactly* the feeling that drove dread into my heart the following morning.

In the full morning light, while recovering from our failed attempt, I was able to really look around at the towering walls above. The magnitude of the remoteness and insanity of the entire adventure really sunk in. It's that moment during a big project or life change in which the commitment level crosses a threshold, and your heart skips a beat.

To give you a sense of the overwhelm, I want you to imagine looking up at a skyscraper—perhaps the Gateway Arch in St. Louis, Missouri, if you have ever stood below it. Twice the height of the Statue of Liberty, taller than the Washington Monument, and roughly half the height of the Empire State Building, the St. Louis Arch is 630 feet tall. The average skyscraper in the United States is around 550 feet tall.

Stretching to the sky above me in every direction on this day were twelve walls over *3000 feet* tall. If you stacked up six Gateway

Arches or average skyscrapers, or two Empire State Buildings on top of each other, they would *almost* reach the summit of the average walls in the area. And these walls are packed into two very small river valleys occupying less than three square miles.

This is when it hit me: the first heavily anxiety-producing moment of *oh-crap* dread. I had to choose the mountain I wanted to climb.

Picking the right mountain on an expedition is tricky, but nowhere near as challenging as doing this in our day-to-day lives. Upon my return to the "real world" after this trip, I had a realization and discovered a single Vertical Lesson that has helped me and teams I've worked with gain more clarity and momentum than any other idea I've ever uncovered.

After settling into the groove of "living in the dirt" as we call it, the euphoria of being in such a beautiful place was washed away by the reality that we faced three significant problems.

First of all, we quickly realized that what we thought would be a mere inconvenience turned out to be a daily routine of misery. Our potato, oatmeal, and ramen diet had grown old by day three, and our bodies started to ache for protein. Fortunately, the Italian mountain guides continued to be quite friendly and felt sorry for us, occasionally feeding us lunch and giving sugar for our tea. Knowing we were short on protein, they donated some canned

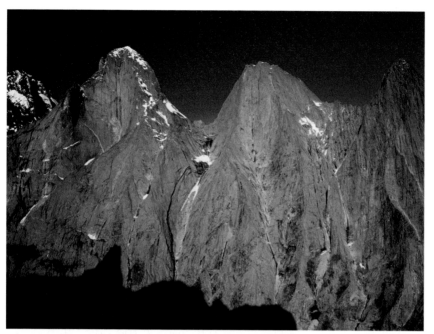

Three walls of the Aksu valley over 3000 feet tall

An inspiring view of the Russian Tower from our basecamp

The Russian Tower with an endless view of unclimbed peaks beyond

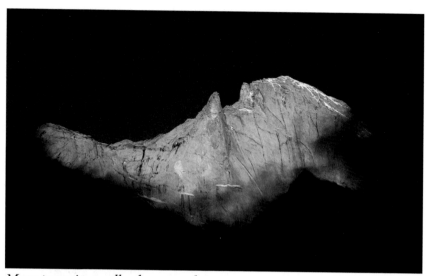

More towering walls above our basecamp

meat protein product. It was essentially Alpo dog food, relabeled. Seriously. It was called "Bill Beef," and was truly disgusting in every way. Choking it down with ramen, it was marginally palatable, and did restore us to a reasonably functioning level.

The food issue would have been easier to stomach had we anything better to do with our time, but thanks to the weather, we didn't. During our days in the Aksu Valley, it rained heavily nine out of ten days, while the temperature hovered between 35 and 45 degrees Fahrenheit. We were tent-bound for days while enduring this miserable weather. And when I say "tent," I don't mean the spacious type you might see a family enjoying in a campground or at your local sports store. Oh no; this was a small, two-person tent that you could barely sit up in. It seemed like a great idea when I bought it, and sure enough, it has kept me alive in mountain ranges around the globe, but it is a miserable space in which to live. Craig's tent was even smaller, and Misha "No Problem's" tent barely passed as a shelter at all. Since my tent was the most storm-worthy shelter,

Me and a delicious can of Bill Beef in front of my tent and our humble base camp in the Aksu Valley

Craig, No Problem and I spent most of our days cramped in it. We passed the time drinking tea and reading when we weren't cooking one of our three carb-heavy meals of the day.

While we ate miserably and watched the limited number of days left in my dream climbing trip drain down the valley, a most critical issue refused resolution. Before we knew it, Craig's time was up. We knew going in that the climbing objectives were well beyond his skill level, but I depended on his keen Third-World navigation skills for survival. After getting thrown in the streets and robbed by police, then the constant threats and machine guns in our faces during our epic journey into the valley, the thought of staying in the Aksu valley without my brother terrified me. My original optimistic plan had me completing a climb with his friend Josh in short order, then returning to Bishkek with Craig when his exit day arrived.

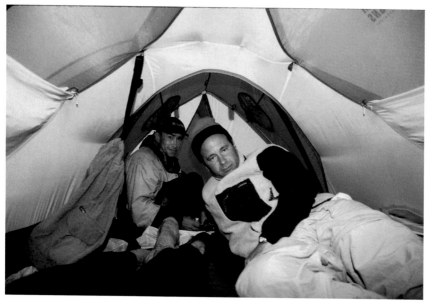

Misha, Craig, and my feet packed into my tent for another day of rain

As you have probably also experienced, the best-made plans often change the moment you get into action.

As Craig's deadline to leave the valley quickly approached, anxiety robbed me of sleep and started to fill my mind with worry nearly every moment. I wrestled with all the possible options, and hung on to one of the few absolutes I knew. If I left with my brother, I definitely would not climb anything.

Sometimes, you have no idea how something might turn out, the choice that keeps your dream alive is the only choice that makes sense.

Risky? Certainly. Uncomfortable? Definitely. Worth it? Absolutely!

Craig and I discussed in detail what the journey without him could be like. We talked at length about whether No Problem could effectively act as my guide through the chaos of the region with truly *no problem*. Craig felt uncomfortable with the idea, but No Problem assured us he could handle it. Although I was hesitant at first, it was No Problem's passion for helping me pursue my dream until the very last moment that led me to take him at his word. In passion there is commitment.

With my primary concern about the logistics of getting home upgraded to at least "reasonable plan in place," my attention then turned to the ultimate crux: finding a partner.

On the morning of July 18th, Craig left me and the beauty of the Aksu Valley behind. His words of advice gave me courage and hope as he put his backpack on and gave me one last hug. Looking deep into my eyes and heart, he assured me, "You're going to be fine, brother. Be safe, climb your mountain, and we will celebrate upon your return to Bishkek. I will be waiting for you." I smiled from ear to ear. I knew he believed, and belief is huge, fueling the courage you need to press on.

Craig and I enjoying the endless walls in the Aksu Valley—our last photo together before his return to Bishkek

I've often said in my keynote speeches that second only to love, belief is the greatest gift you can give someone. When you give both, it makes a huge difference in those you connect with, even strangers.

At this point I was eighteen days into my expedition and still did not have a climbing partner lined up. The Italian team had a new route objective they were focused on, and there were no other teams in the Aksu Valley. I had been doing my best to convince Andre, the Russian climber who was logistical support for the Italian team, to partner with me. The "this is my life dream" story that had worked on the airlines and other hurdles I surmounted garnered his best intentions, but the bottom line was, he was busy working to support the Italian expedition. Even then, Andre strung me along with possibility; "Manley, maybe day after tomorrow, we can climb something." But the day after tomorrow came and went, and came and went.

Then the sun came and stayed. As the barometer rose on my Suunto adventure watch, so did my frustration. On my CD Walkman, I listened to Bob Marley's "Waiting in Vain," wondering if I would ever find a climbing partner.

20/20 Hindsight

As I was reading through my journal in preparing this book, my stomach flipped as I read the entry from July 19th:

Am I waiting in vain for Andre? Another sunny day passes with no climbing. Tomorrow I must climb with or without Andre.

I will attempt a solo (ascent) of the Central Pyramid if Andre does not climb with me, but I will still need him to show me where the route starts.

I was ready to attempt a climb by myself in the middle of central Asia. My stomach flipped when I read that because knowing what I know now, I look back on that thought as bold and terrifying. I also look back realizing it was only slightly crazier than what unfolded next.

Andre rolled into the camp with a huge smile that evening. "Manley! I have someone for you to meet! This is Jula and Dima. They come from Moscow to climb, and they are strong. Very experienced, and they want to talk to you about maybe climb with you!"

Yes!

I was desperate, and this was at least a chance. We began a long and drawn-out conversation that went on for hours. The normal process would have taken perhaps one or two days to share our climbing experiences, get to know each other, and then climb some short routes together. This would have given us time to understand our styles, to build our communication protocols, and to develop trust before we committed to the unknown Vertical towering above us. All of this, however, was severely hindered by two factors. Number one: Dima spoke about ten words of English, and his lovely wife, Jula, spoke about 50. Number two: my looming deadline to leave the valley. The following day was my *commit to The Vertical or don't climb* deadline.

They shared a sense of urgency to get climbing immediately; that much we agreed on. Just that small moment of decision—the declaration of *when it shall begin*—gave us an incredible amount of focus, setting a powerful force of energy in motion.

Jula quickly emerged as a sweet and caring friend, smiling often, especially when she spoke of her and Dima's children in Moscow. Her stunning blue eyes balanced strength and confidence with care and concern. Within minutes, I felt a connection with her heart as she committed to helping me realize my dream of climbing a massive wall in Kyrgyzstan. She said, "Manley, we can live on the wall for days and nights. We will not stop until we summit." Now, that lit me up!

Jula contemplating The Vertical while sipping some hot tea

Meanwhile, Dima remained stoic and silent, his stern demeanor never giving way to even a smile. He was so serious. What he lacked in people-focused warmth, his energy seemed to make up for in raw, uncompromising perseverance. Of course, I hadn't seen him climb anything yet, but I had an immediate gut feeling about him; *this guy is tougher than nails.* I just knew he was willing to suffer; there was no doubt in my mind. Especially in the remote mountains of Kyrgyzstan, I figured what he might lack in feel-good, he could make up for with ass-kicking resilience.

Dima in another stoic stare

Dima mostly stared, I mostly talked, and Jula mostly smiled. After more than an hour, Dima broke his verbal fast by abruptly, saying, "Manley, you skinny!" It makes me laugh now, but it caught me off guard then. I tried not to take offense, and said, "Yes, Dima, but I am strong and will not give up until summit!"

"Hmm," is all I got in return.

As our conversation approached the two-hour mark, Dima broke his silence abruptly once again. "Manley, let's climb! Da, Manley."

A committed decision to actually climb together—yes! Finally!

Now, what mountain to climb? It was time to *Declare Our Current Climb.*

There were many route options, but Andre had one recommendation he suggested that might be reasonable. *Reasonable* is a relative adjective here, as every wall and every route in the region demands a full range of expert climbing skills. Competency is an obvious prerequisite, and your ability to persevere with a steel core of resilience is mandatory. The difference between success and mere ambition depends on a maniacal commitment to live for days outside of your comfort zone. It's no exaggeration to say the truth is that the entire dream was beyond the fringes of sanity for most. Only the boldest and most experienced climbers need even consider committing to a multiday alpine big wall expedition in such a remote region. The truth is, we had no assurance of success, nor even a guarantee that we'd even make it back alive. To attempt one of the few "reasonable" routes was the least I could do to calm the ever-present churning anxiety within me.

"Yes, Manley, Dima, Jula. I think this is best." Andre pointed to the northwest, downriver from our base camp, as he called it out to us with a poetic flair: "This one, *The Northwest Pillar of the Central Pyramid. Also we call Peak Aksu 3850.*" Wow, even the name sounded bad-ass.

I grinned and repeated the name: "The Northwest Pillar of the Central Pyramid of the Aksu Valley, Kyrgyzstan. Yes, that should do!"

The Northwest Pillar of the Central Pyramid of the Aksu Valley, aka *peak 3850, Kyrgyzstan*

I stared off into the thin air high above where Andre had pointed. We couldn't see the wall from our camp, but my words seemed to follow Andre's gesture into The Vertical above. In that moment, our minds ascended up into The Vertical, and at once we were all silent as we imagined our own version of life surviving on the edge, and what our days ahead might be like.

Imagine Your Summit

This is such a powerful moment; one in which we rarely take enough time to truly leverage when setting goals. Ask questions so you know and feel what the experience of success will be like.

"What's the summit like, Andre?" I asked. "Beauty, Manley. All beauty, all ways you can see, Manley. So many mountains, so much more than you can see from here. You will be happy on summit. Yes, Manley."

Even in Andre's broken English, the power of his description ignited our imaginations. Standing there in the stillness, time seemed to pause as the spell of the summit swept us up. It stirred our souls and took our pre-climb energy and focus to yet another level.

In the Batken market, I had purchased a child's school notebook to use as a journal. The paper was rough and inconsistent, somewhere between handmade paper and an old notebook that had survived a flood. We opened my crude journal to the blank middle, and Andre began to draw our map, known as the topo, or topographical map. Andre's verbal memory and description of the route was detailed and clear, but his drawing skills were not. He sketched a rough image of the overall mountain and added a few more pen strokes to indicate the way of the Northwest Pillar route. It was better than nothing, but the equivalent of drawing a couple of odd shapes, and then a few lines to illustrate how you get from New York City to Dallas.

Andre then got to work describing the route in detail for us, drawing another crude topo. He left long sections of Vertical as just a single line on the paper: he instructed us to "just climb, up, up—climb crack until find place to sleep." Oh, yeah, the *place to sleep* part.

I was very concerned about having at least two locations on the wall to make a hanging camp in The Vertical where we could sleep, eat and recover enough to continue on the next day. This was another critical decision-point. I had dragged my luxurious hanging tent, known as a portaledge, halfway around the world, and there it sat beside us. All thirteen pounds of it.

I'm not sure if that sounds like much weight, but let me just say when it's one more bulky item strapped to your back as you grind your way up a remote alpine big wall, you think twice before bringing it. If we were to add thirteen more pounds, wouldn't more food and water be a more logical choice? Or should we bring a modern mountain shelter that could ensure our ability to endure whatever weather and logistics we encountered in the days ahead? One thing was clear; both were not an option. We would either skimp on food and water, or shelter. Would we need the portable hanging ledge and be sorry and miserable if we left it behind? Andre said there were at least one or two good ledges and we did not need it. I don't think Dima and Jula ever seriously considered bringing it, slickly dismissing it as a western climbing luxury. "We don't need hotel; our mind strong, Manley. Tent, only tent." Dima was very excited about taking their tent as our only shelter. It was a rare occasion for him to get excited, so I trusted that their two-person tent would be adequate for us.

Just after midnight, we finished packing everything we thought we needed to survive on the wall for three days. Our food and water supplies were minimal, leaving us enough for two light meals a day and less than two liters of water per person, per day. I felt comfortable with our essential climbing gear decisions. We agreed to take thirty pieces of gear to protect the leader and build anchors, but I met great resistance from Dima and Jula around simple choices about supporting equipment. Supporting equipment includes items like flashlights, sleeping and shelter choices, a small first aid kit, and duct tape. Many of these items are default equipment when I climb with Western partners and require no debate. Take light, for example. Typically, it is standard for every team member to have a headlamp for hands-free operations in the dark, and we also bring a backup for the team. Not Dima and Jula. They wanted to bring one headlamp only, for the entire team to share. I just flat-out refused and told them they could share one if they wished, but I was going to have one just for me, dedicated to my use. After twenty minutes presenting my case in broken English, I could not convince them to each bring one, so they committed to sharing a second headlamp between them.

Reflecting on that evening now, I realize that the process of preparing for our launch into The Vertical did not build my confidence as I might have expected. There were just too many unknowns. We tried to get comfortable with as many variables as we could, but ultimately, at some point, we just had to go forward with what we knew. What I *did* have was courage, and Dima and Jula also seemed to have a double-sized tank overflowing with courage on tap for us to draw from.

Don't Wait for Confidence

This insight became more clear for me after hearing my friend, Deirdre Van Nest, deliver a keynote speech in 2014. Deirdre really emphasized the importance of not waiting to act until you feel you have enough confidence. Instead, she encourages us to focus on building courage.

Don't wait for confidence. If I had waited for confidence, I would still be dreaming about that climb. What I've learned in the mountains, business, and life is to commit first. Next, develop your courage and competence to step up and embrace the exposure. Confidence comes as a byproduct of courageous experiences.

Before the light of dawn, we would get on with it, together, with courage, some food, and just enough English to get us by.

Little did I know my courage would be put to the test before we even stepped up into The Vertical.

Vertical Momentum: From Insight to Action

Climbing is easier than what you are trying to accomplish in your life every day. Think I'm crazy? I honestly believe this for several reasons.

Number one is that climbing demands a unique clarity of purpose and an outright declaration of focus. In the mountains, you must Declare a Current Climb or you will get nowhere. After all, you can only climb one mountain at a time. This is easy compared to what we deal with in our day-to-day lives.

You tell me: Are you trying to climb just one mountain in your life, or do you feel like you are facing multiple mountains?

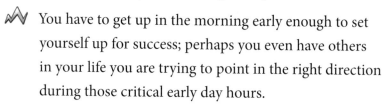 You have to get up in the morning early enough to set yourself up for success; perhaps you even have others in your life you are trying to point in the right direction during those critical early day hours.

Next, you must engage in your work, and show up with the attitude and physical presence that your team and others you work with expect.

Now you have to bring the goods and deliver beyond exceptions. Catch up on hundreds of emails. Add in phone calls, voice mail, and hours of meetings. Move some key initiatives forward. Before you know it, the day has slipped away and you are rushing to get out the door.

After some end-of-day responsibilities are addressed, you walk through the door of your home, hoping you'll have something left over for those who need you most.

But you still have to figure out dinner and perhaps some last-minute work.

Oh, yeah; you still need to squeeze in some exercise and try to avoid drinking or yelling at anyone you really care about.

Just thinking about it all wears me out!

Have you ever attended a great keynote speech or workshop? Or perhaps inspiration came from a good book, a sermon, or a mentor. But you know it when you hear it; an amazing and actionable idea that you believe will make a difference for you, your team and organization. If you are like me, you get pretty fired up, especially if the idea was delivered in a way that inspired you to immediately take action. Perhaps you even took great notes and were completely committed to action. Next, you walked out the door with the best of intentions. Fast-forward three months and you are stuck in the exact same place you were when you were first enlightened by the idea. Sucks, huh? I know. I've been there too many times to count.

The *Declare Your Current Climb* strategy will ensure this doesn't happen to you. When you use it consistently and with intention, you will gain significant momentum and actually make progress on ideas that you know will help you grow and advance. Next you will learn how to put this strategy into action in three steps. We are going to lay down a foundational rule, then help you gain clarity and choose a Current Climb that makes the biggest impact in the fastest timeframe. And finally, most importantly, you're going to gain several tactical tools to help you build and maintain momentum on your Current Climb so that you can realize results faster.

Clarity Paves the Path of Consistency

1. Declare Only One Initiative as Your Current Climb

"But Manley, I already have multiple mountains that I'm trying to climb; why only one?" Picking one is essential for that very reason: the fact that you are already dealing with the pressure of trying to keep your head above the sea of overwhelm with the mountains you are facing in your life. Knowing you can't ignore the other mountains and regular responsibilities you already are committed to, how can you expect adding a new list of initiatives will lead to any success? I've fallen into that trap over and over; trying to add more without first stepping back to take an honest look at everything I was already committed to, and then adding multiple new initiatives to my list. When we try to add more than one initiative that we know is going to truly improve and make a difference, our ambition undermines our focus, which in turn undermines our momentum. Then we just give up on the entire list because we simply have too much to maintain already. This is easy, and we may even feel it is justified. "Well, that new project, seminar, book, sermon, meeting...it *was* a great idea, and I know it would really help if I implemented that, but I'm simply too busy!" Having the clarity to commit to one, and only one *Current Climb* gives you laser focus and ensures that what's truly important gets traction.

2. Select Your Current Climb

Now, *which one* to pick? Strategically selecting your current climb is a critical step. When you reflect on ideas, opportunities or project seeds you've recently encountered, which ones really jumped out at you? Which ones stirred your passion and got you fired up? Maybe it even evoked a head nod or made you open your eyes wide and sit up. You know, that deep visceral sense of interest when a good idea hits you. If you don't already have a way to identify super-hot, actionable ideas as you hear them, I would encourage you to start doing so when taking notes. Use something to identify them inline. (For me, it's a star with a circle around it, and also an "A" for *action* and a circle around it.) Another simple but powerful tactic is to keep significant ideas you want to act upon on a separate piece of paper. Then review your notes within a week of the *aha!* moment during a regular planning session.

Here's the next tactical tip: When you are reviewing your list, be aware of your emotional response to ideas that you identified as *aha-actionable* in the moment. Now do you notice reluctance to implement? This is the heavy pull of gravity trying to keep you on the ground, and it could be a sign that the idea has the potential for massive impact for you. Being a climber, I have become keenly aware of the force of gravity. We know it is a constant on earth, but like time, our perception of how hard gravity is pulling down on us is highly subjective. Have you ever noticed that some days just getting out of bed feels like someone has literally cranked up the gravity setting for the day? Your body, arms, legs, thoughts, and even your words feel heavier, weighted down as you drag through your day. And then, some days it feels like you are running on the moon, with a strong wind at your back. That is the **Emotional Gravity**. Developing inner awareness of your sense of gravity is key. Watch out for items that seem to increase gravity by dragging you down and distracting you; dreaded small projects or activities that are consuming energy and perhaps creating anxiety, ultimately robbing your full focus. Occasionally, the best Current Climb option for you could be to catch up on or knock out one of these items. I know it's hard to declare a single current climb, so as you are evaluating your potential, feel free to maintain a Current Climb Queue and know that you aren't saying "no" to a bigger initiative—just no for right now.

You can use the following list to quickly evaluate a potential Current Climb. The greater the number of items that ring true as you consider the initiative, the more seriously you should consider it as your Current Climb:

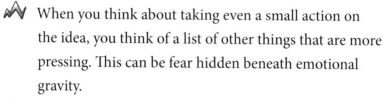

- When you think about taking even a small action on the idea, you think of a list of other things that are more pressing. This can be fear hidden beneath emotional gravity.

- It is a barrier that stands in your way of accomplishing other goals, initiatives, or needed change, and could act as a domino or clear the path for other progress.

- In a safe state of mind in which you are inspired, courageous, or reflecting, it stands out as worth pursuing.

- It's of high importance (may or may not have high urgency).

- It is something at least on the edge of your comfort zone.

- You know it could lead to breakthrough results in one or more areas of your life.

- You understand why it is worth pursuing; it is emotionally palpable and crystal clear.

Once you pick just one Current Climb, the final step is to declare with commitment and conviction. It helps to at least say it to yourself and write down, "*No matter what*, I'm going to move this forward every day."

3. Build and Maintain Momentum

Ideas are Free; Execution is Priceless Scott Ginsberg (2011)

Selecting a single Current Climb is the easy part. Building and maintaining *momentum* is the ultimate crux of implementing this Vertical Lesson.

The first key to building momentum is focusing on your Current Climb first, before the storm of chaos sets in. As soon as possible, ideally before you check email or engage in meetings and other daily activities, sit down and take a small action to move your Current Climb forward. Do it first.

The second key to keep your momentum going is to do something *every single day* to move your Current Climb forward, no matter what. Sounds easy, but building new habits is a critical failure point in the adoption of new desired behaviors and routines.

Knowing that installing new habits is a key to realizing results, I've searched for decades for the magic answer to how we can change our behaviors. In 2012, I discovered the work of BJ Fogg, Ph.D., a behavioral scientist and professor at the Stanford Graduate School of Business. Dr. Fogg is recognized as a leading expert in changing human behavior. His work stood out to me for two reasons; it is very practical and immediately actionable, and most importantly, he's achieved remarkable results. His techniques work. Dr. Fogg discovered that when people attached a new habit to an existing routine, they were much more likely to create a lasting habit.

Here's a simple but extremely effective way to leverage this breakthrough idea in your life. Let's say that every day, you come in and make your coffee, tea, or fill up your water bottle. Without fail, you execute that routine. What I would encourage you to do is take a simple sticky note, write your Current Climb on it, then rubber-band that to the side of your cup or bottle. Now, every time you make your drink, as well as when you drink from it, you will be reminded to execute a small step toward your Current Climb.

The third key to build momentum is to know that as little as five minutes of effort towards your Current Climb can build incredible momentum. This is counterintuitive, as we believe we have to spend significant time, even hours to move important initiatives forward. The problem with carving out extensive periods of time is that in the long run, it's not realistic. It's just a matter of time before you say "well, I just don't have time to work on my Current Climb today with everything else I have going on." But you always have five minutes. If you can work on your Current Climb for up to twenty minutes, go for it. Beware of trying to carve out large chunks of time. When you feel more internal resistance, reduce the amount of time you focus on your Current Climb. I've also found using a timer to be very effective. Set it for five to twenty minutes and notice how working against the clock cranks up your focus.

4. Visibility Drives Velocity

Keep your Current Climb visible. I recommend leveraging old-school tools and modern technology to keep your Current Climb in your face. Using technology, schedule a standing calendar event, a recurring task, or even project management software. Change your smartphone wallpaper to something related to your Current Climb. For old-school tools, the sticky note is still a favorite. Write your Current Climb on multiple sticky notes and try placing them on your monitor or laptop, your alarm clock, your mirror, your dashboard, or any other spot that is visible in your day-to-day life. It might drive your partner crazy, but it is worth it.

CHAPTER 5

Vertical Lesson 3: Get On Belay!

The morning came early and cold in the shadows of the towering walls above. Fueled more by excitement than anxiety, we made our final supply check and left the relative comfort of our base camp a few hours after daybreak. Jula established a fast pace ahead of us while Dima and I marched down the valley, burdened by all of the equipment and supplies we needed to live on the wall for three days. Despite the weight of our physical load, our spirits were high as the sun began to light the roaring Aksu River beside us.

I only recall a handful of essential Russian words from my days in central Asia, two of which Dima shouted over and over to me as he pointed to the wall above: "Da!"(yes) and "Nyet!" (no). Dima motioned toward our intended route as he walked and blurted sentence after sentence of colorful Russian, peppered with "Da, Manley! Da!" and "Nyet, nyet, Manley!"

Dima began to speed up and then slow his pace erratically, then froze in time with his right hand pointed to blue sky above. I remember being very confused and thinking, "What is he doing?" Something was wrong. I felt like I was watching a slow-motion movie as Dima's entire body wrenched and fell backwards. Suddenly, I realized his head was about to crash into the jagged boulders between us. At the last possible moment, I dove out with my hands fully extended, barely catching the back of his head and cradling it to the ground as he collapsed in a grand-mal seizure.

"Jula!" I yelled at the top of my lungs.

Jula ran back to us and helped me roll Dima's stiff, convulsing body onto his side. I frantically covered him with my jacket while Jula held his hand and head. After three agonizing minutes, Dima slipped into something just short of a coma; he was out cold.

On the edge of absolute panic, I stared into Jula's blue eyes and asked, "Is Dima OK? What do we do, Jula? Is he OK?"

"Manley, Dima fine!" she proclaimed confidently, without hesitation.

Huh? I remember thinking, "Whoa. I don't know where you are from, but where I come from, he needs help! We are three days from a third-world hospital!"

Jula went on to try and assure me. "Don't worry, Manley, no problem. Dima, one seizure, one year. No more seizure, Dima, one year."

Do you know why I was completely freaking out? Guess who was going to hold my rope in his hands as I led us into The Vertical unknown? Dima was to belay me as I climbed, and I was to belay Dima when it was his turn to take the rope higher on the wall.

The belay is a technique by which a person holds the rope for another while he or she climbs. The belay is a critical part of exploring The Vertical, as it establishes a margin of safety for the climber and literally puts the climber's life in the hands of the belayer. The belayer is the person who is intensely focused on using the belay technique, also known as being *on belay*. In rock climbing, a metal device is typically used to belay with. It allows a person to effortlessly lock the rope off with friction when a climber falls, arresting their fall and minimizing the chance of injury.

Effective belayers must do a few things exceptionally well. They must provide the climber just enough rope for them to move upward without giving them too much slack, which could result in them falling too far. The belayer must also take care to not hold the climber too tight, preventing progress and possibly causing a fall. And most critically, the belayer must be extremely present and communicate consistently with the climber, be alert and ready to provide more or less rope as needed, and when the climber falls, must instantly lock off the rope. Locking off the rope is a simple shift of the hand with the rope, which allows the belay device to apply friction, locking the rope to stop it from sliding through the belay device.

While Dima rested, I began to drown in doubt as I continued to face what seemed to be the most difficult decision of my life. Could I trust Jula's confidence in Dima's health and ability? I must have asked her at least ten times. Again and again I looked into her eyes, "Jula, Dima belay me, no problem?"

"Manley, I say again and again! Dima no problem. He good belay. Manley, Dima only one seizure, one year. Dima no more seizure one year, probably."

Probably?"

Did she just say *probably?*

My head swimming in anxiety, confusion, and desire, her broken English began to blur my judgment even more. "Jula, can you say that again? Did you say no problem, or *probably? Maybe* no more seizure, or, *no more seizure?*"

After seventy minutes, Dima started moving, began drinking water, and eventually was back on his feet. During a prolonged stretch of silence, Dima became re-energized as he focused his eyes again and again on the summit of the Central Pyramid.

Finally, Dima's voice broke the tension with confidence and force as he pointed up to the sky blanketed above the jagged summit of the Central Pyramid.

"*Summit!* Manley! I feel good! I strong, Manley! Let's climb!"

(I know what you are thinking: "Are you going to tell me that you went climbing with those Russians, Manley?")

Sometimes desire and commitment beyond circumstance drives us beyond any comfort zone we could possibly imagine. Staring into both of their souls, beyond our language barrier, beyond my fears and questions, I did something we all must do from time to time. I went with my gut. I trusted them.

With more than enough reasons for retreat before we even began, we carefully discussed scenarios and how we would deal with any of us being unable to climb. Considering all of our options, and *focusing on facts instead of fear*, we all stood together and resumed our approach to the base of Aksu 3850, recommitted to climb the Northwest Pillar of The Central Pyramid.

Little did we know, Dima's seizure was just the beginning of our dance with gravity, fear, and fate.

Vertical Momentum: From Insight to Action

In climbing, the belay process is absolutely critical. It is the difference between life and death, safe passage to the summit and utter disaster. It is the foremost element of trust in a climbing partner; if you have a shadow of doubt about your belayer, it undermines every thought and move you make in The Vertical. Trusting your belayer is crucial before you take your first step upward toward the summit.

The mechanics of the belay process are deceptively simple. The results of its application in The Vertical, and in life, are profound.

There are a few points that you need to be aware of to understand how the belay allows climbers to safely accomplish what appears to be impossible. Likewise, the very same principle can be your secret weapon in life to help you stretch your own comfort zone and reach toward summits you have yet to even imagine.

The person who *belays* you is your *belayer*. The belay mechanisms are simple and only require awareness and consistent execution of six principles to enable safe progress towards your summit.

1. With most climbing styles, *we expect to fall* and put systems in place to allow for our mistakes. The belay is the heart of the safety system in which your partner literally has your life in his/her hands. Do you have processes in place to allow for your inevitable mistakes? Simple systems to arrest your falls? If not, step one is to **get a belayer in place.**

2. Your belayer must **feed just enough rope** to enable your climb into the unknown. Do your partners give you enough rope to climb? Enough space to grow?

3. Your belayer must at the same time **avoid giving you *too much* rope**. If a partner gives you too much slack, when you do fall, the impact is greater—increasing the risks for both.

4. Likewise, your belayer must be **careful to not hold you back**. They must feed you just enough rope as you move. Identifying a *belayer* who is holding you back in life and disconnecting from them can be one of the most courageous and productive actions you will ever take.

5. Most importantly, when you fall (and you will if you are regularly reaching beyond your comfort zone to your true potential), your belayer must immediately **lock off your rope** to stop your fall. This is the moment of truth. Your belayer must remain intensely present and ready to quickly arrest your fall to minimize the impact. Are your partners *fully present* when you're connected to them?

6. After a fall, your belayer **focuses on reassurance**, helping you recover and get back on the wall as soon as possible. Once the terror of a fall gives way to the realization that your partner has saved you from any unrecoverable damage, you can quickly begin to climb again. Soon you will find yourself at your previous high-point, moving beyond it with the assurance of your belay.

So, how do you implement these principles in your day-to-day life? Don't let their simplicity distract you from their power and the results they will bring you. When executed *consistently* in your life, the *On Belay* lesson will have a dramatic impact on your results.

I invite you to get into action with the Belay principle in just five minutes a day, leveraging three simple steps. Every day of your life, in your moment of awareness, start with two essential questions:

1. Who Do *I Need On Belay* Today?

To accomplish everything, you have your sights on—your current climb, the myriad tasks and demands you are juggling, the chaos of your daily life and efforts to realize your potential— what person can you commit to reach out to and mutually *serve*? Whom do *you need On Belay*? Note that while you are intentionally connecting with the person *you need On Belay*, you are *proactively* offering to serve them.

Watch out for the excuse I give myself most often: "Well, I'm busy today" or, "I don't want to bug them." Ridiculous! We take time to communicate via most of those channels every day with many people. The difference here is that you are strategically, intentionally, and consistently *On Belay* for the person *you* need most.

2. Who Will *I Belay* Today?

This question helps you strategically focus on the one individual that needs *your* support most today. It could be a fellow team member, your boss, business colleague, or client. Do not limit yourself by the vertical or horizontal boundaries of your organization; again, do a quick check-in with them, using the phrase you feel most comfortable with, via the channel they are most attuned to, and that you have minimal resistance to using at that moment.

A common resistance I get from people is, "what do you mean, 'connect with people?' I'm overwhelmed with email and phone calls, you name it. Manley, I'm connecting all day!" The key difference is that when you *Get On Belay*, the connection is outbound and initiated by you. The true power of the belay comes from you being strategic and intentional in your belay efforts. When people in your life know you have them *On Belay*, they feel it in the sincere and consistent connections you make with them. Over time, the effect is profound and results will show up in ways you can't imagine.

Know that giving equal focus and effort to both the people you need *On Belay* and to those who need you is essential. Upon reflection, people will often find that they may be providing a solid belay for others while not building the belays they need. Also, some people observe that they are connected to many every day who need them, but not in a deep, intentional, and meaningful way as the belay calls for. Of all the lessons you pick up in our time together, none will have a greater, more lasting impact on you and on those in your life than the belay, but only if you execute the final step.

3. Get On Belay!

This is the easy part: reach out and connect. In-person, human connection trumps all and is ideal, but don't let that get in the way of *Getting On Belay* every day. Text, email, social media, phone, video or in person—just connect! And don't overthink what you say when you reach out. Try a simple question like, "how are you?" Or let them know "I'm thinking of you." It doesn't take long and is *worth it*.

Remember that being *On Belay* is about you being intentional about who *you* need *On Belay, and* who needs you *On Belay*, every day.

Strategic, intentional, consistent connection.

CHAPTER 6

Vertical Lesson 4: Challenge Your Beliefs

Between the thin air at 10,000 feet above sea level and slogging our gear up the steep approach, I felt exhausted before we ever started climbing. Finally reaching the base of the wall by late morning, we rested for a quick sip of water, got our climbing gear on, and launched into The Vertical.

Like most big projects, we got started later than expected. We made good time through the afternoon and cranked past the first 500 feet of the route using only our hands and feet to move up the wall on lead, our ropes and equipment only providing a safety net should we fall. By early evening, we landed on the first good ledge along our route. A hanging island in the sky, the eight-by-six-feet of rare horizontal surface was a huge relief. There was enough room to set up Dima and Jula's tent and still a few extra feet to move around. In The Vertical world of big walls, a ledge is a very welcomed feature, and quite rare on most adventures.

Dima had climbed with focus and power the first day. Jula struggled to follow us up our ropes with the heavy pack containing our supplies, but showed her unrelenting determination and drive in the initial twenty feet off the ground. It didn't take long to see their resilience in action, and they didn't fail to meet my expectations.

While I started to grow more confident in Dima's health and Vertical abilities, a different concern developed. I noticed the two approached several basic safety protocols differently than my partners and I from the West. To move the team up the wall, usually one person takes the end of a rope and ties it to his or her harness, then leads the rope up into the unknown. During the climb, the leader places metal tools into the wall that will help stop the climber should he or she fall. All the while, the belayer and any other team members encourage from below and do their best to stay warm and motivated.

When the leader runs out of rope or reaches a good place to stop (typically somewhere between 150 and 200 feet up) an anchor is built. The anchor is a point where you arrange three or four metal devices to connect you and your equipment to the wall. The leader then gets on belay and brings up the team. The anchor is a key point—a milestone where you reassess your direction, refuel your body and mind, and rebuild momentum. Staying attached to the anchor point is an essential and basic safety step.

Imagine you are standing on top of your kitchen table with me, and your kitchen table is perched 570 feet off the ground. We have built our anchor; it is holding us to the wall. You need to attach yourself to the anchor with a metal clip you've probably seen (See photo) it's called a carabiner. (There are two types of carabiners: nonlocking, meaning the gate can open and close easily, and locking, which have a small sleeve that you easily and quickly screw shut. This simple mechanism prevents the gate from opening accidentally.) So, *you* are attached to our anchor with a single *locking* carabiner.

Dima's locking carabiner

Would *you* take two seconds to lock the carabiner shut?

Of course!

As a general rule, I (and most other Western climbers I know) typically use *two* separate locking carabiners to stay attached to anchors at all times.

Not Dima.

As soon as I noticed this, I said "Dima—you need to lock your carabiner!"

"Manley, not necessary!"

What?

Dima at our first ledge at the end of day one. You can see his locking carabiner in front of his right shin.

I then looked at Jula's carabiner. Same scenario.

She was hanging 570 feet off the ground, attached to the wall with only one carabiner, and did *not* have the gate locked.

"Jula, you have to lock your carabiner; you could come unclipped and fall!"

Jula responded in a sweeter tone of voice, but the message was the same.

"Manley, *really,* not necessary!"

Wow.

I kept telling them they needed to lock their carabiners. Over and over, I repeated my concern that they needed to do it. Then I just started doing it for them, reaching over and screwing the gate lock for them. Eventually, after several anchors, they would see me coming and reluctantly screw the gate shut, just so I wouldn't aggravate them about it. They were complying, at best, but I know they didn't *believe* it was necessary.

Within moments of getting our tent set up, a light rain started. Dread. When you are committed to the climb, any funky weather always puts an extra layer of fear in your heart. Would it stop our climb? What if we decided to climb higher the next day and the weather got worse? I started to imagine the horror of being stranded high on the wall, cramped three into a two-person tent, starving and freezing to death. That's when I called on an old familiar friend. Procrastination. With awareness of my mind running down that path of fear, I stepped back and told myself, then our team, "we can't worry about the weather or tomorrow, now we must rest and prepare. In the morning we will see." Procrastinating worry is a wonderful tool. Try it. Put off the worry. Tell the voice of fear, "not now, we can talk later." In this case, it was "sleep now, worry later."

Vertical Momentum: From Insight to Action

Have you ever had to gain compliance in your life or business? With Dima and Jula and their carabiners, I was *chasing the behavior*, first by telling the person what I needed, over and over. Then I get tired of telling them, right? So I started doing it for them, hoping they would learn by watching and finally *get it*.

This insight contains the power to help you make dramatic leaps in the results you achieve. At first, this path may feel like it is more work on the front-end. It is. The results are not only more sustainable, they are also significantly more impactful to long-term momentum and success. I look back now and wonder how much faster I could have gotten not just compliance, but commitment if I had challenged Dima and Jula's beliefs about their safety systems.

Can telling a person what you want, need, and expect work? Definitely. Is leading by example often effective? Absolutely. But if these are the only two methods you have to lead with, you are going to miss out on a massive opportunity to get the results you want much faster. I've done this over and over in business and also in raising my kids. It took me fifteen years before I really understood what I was doing and why it took so long to even get compliance from my Russian partners on this simple lesson.

Stop chasing behaviors; start challenging beliefs.

A simple question can be extraordinarily powerful. "Why do you believe you don't need to lock your carabiner?" I think asking that question would have been a game changer.

The next time you notice a behavior that you believe is not driving the results you want, instead of trying to chase the behavior into compliance, ask yourself or the person who is demonstrating the behavior, what belief is driving the action or choice. I found myself chasing behaviors in business all too often—even simple operational behaviors, like following a process or using a recommended tool.

I was involved in a massive multimillion-dollar business project. We had rolled out a new tool that revolutionized how our employees accessed critical business information across the organization. The rollout and technology were delivered within scope and by all measures had exceeded expectations. The only problem was people were not using it; we did not get the behavior we expected or desired. At first, we sent more communications about how important it was for them to use it and how we wanted them to use it. We had leaders in the organization demonstrate using it, step-by-step. Finally we asked our people, "why do you believe it's not necessary to use the new system?" Many expressed their belief that it was too hard to use and not any better than the old way. This insight enabled us to focus our efforts on specifically shifting their perspective of the new system to believing it was easier and better. Before we knew it, people throughout the organization shifted their beliefs about the new system, and mass adoption quickly followed.

In work and life, it is too easy to slip into a habit of chasing behaviors, as managing the behaviors we see in ourselves and others *is* a fundamental part of managing our lives. Managing is not leading. Effective leadership requires us to look beneath the surface of the behavior at beliefs and internal drivers.

CHAPTER 7

Vertical Lesson 5: Ask The Right Questions

On the second morning of our climb, I woke up at 5:00 a.m. I barely peeked my head out and saw wet rock everywhere. The conditions helped me rationalize sleep until 7:00 a.m., hoping the weather would stabilize and the rock dry. If it did, we would have no reason to not boldly carry on, making a major commitment to the massive wall above us.

Sleeping two more hours was a choice I would later regret. As dawn arrived, the weather was overcast and cold but stable, handing us no excuse to turn back. Throughout the night, another thought that had played through my mind was if the weather worsened, we could probably escape to the ground from the ledge. We also knew this point on the climb was likely the last opportunity for a reasonable retreat, requiring a significant recommitment if we agreed to climb on. After a traverse onto the north face of the Central Pyramid, the route threaded us through an intimidating chimney and a wide crack through a roof. Andre had warned that it was the most difficult passage of the route, the crux. More concerning was the realization that this would be the mental commitment crux too. We knew that once we battled through that pitch of climbing and emerged from the wet chimney onto the headwall, we would be making a deeper commitment to our summit.

 Traverse means to move laterally, typically not making much vertical progress. When traversing, it may seem like you are not making progress, since you are not moving up, but progress comes in many ways. Sometimes a shift or change in direction is more important than continuing on in the same way.

Chimney refers to a wide crack on a wall that is big enough for the climber to fit the body into. Chimneys can be very difficult to ascend, requiring a unique set of techniques that leverage the entire body. In many scenarios, they are hard to protect against a leader fall, requiring exceptional focus and confidence for the leader to pass safely.

Crux is the word used to identify the most difficult section or element of a climb.

By the time we got moving that morning, our decision required almost no conversation. We acknowledged that conditions looked stable and that it was time to climb on.

Dima tied into the rope and stepped away from the security of our ledge, climbed onto the delicate face above, then traversed beneath the chimney. Above him, the wall formed into a four-foot-wide chimney dripping with cold water. He was able to place a few pieces of gear in the rock to protect his struggle, then claw his way up into the chimney. As soon as he got his body up into the dark and wet void, he began to slip and was challenged with the fear we climbers face in such moments. He was ten feet above his last piece of gear; meaning a fall at this point would send him flying more than twenty feet down, grating across the coarse granite below. With my focused belay and by pulling in some rope quickly, I could most likely keep him from colliding with our ledge, but the margin of error was slim. Dima yelled in Russian to Jula, and Jula would try to translate as best she could to help me understand if he needed more rope or was about to fall. Based on the tone of his voice and Jula's stress level, I was ready for a massive fall and encouraged him to hang on. He managed to place a piece of gear deep in the back of the chimney just as he fell. It was enough to limit his fall to less than ten feet. He was safe, but shaken up by his desperate effort.

I encouraged him to take his time and recover, but his indomitable spirit only allowed him to rest for a few moments. Within minutes, Dima had remounted The Vertical bull ride and used a colorful assortment of grunting and unknown Russian words to miraculously pass through the crux, squeezing his way past a narrow section of rock that seemed to reach out and grab for every dangling item on his harness to slow his progress. Just as he thought he was free, he would get caught up, the disruption to his momentum nearly sending him into a freefall back into the wet void below him. After a solid hour of exerting energy near his limit,

Dima managed to reach a one-foot by two-and-a-half-foot stance. I call it a "stance" because a "ledge" would be too generous and imply something we could all stand on and relax for a moment. Definitely not. This was more like a small protrusion on the wall that allowed for each of us to have one or two feet planted for a few minutes at a time so we could take some weight off our harnesses, which were grinding into our backs. This required us to hang practically on top of each other, shoulder to shoulder, smashed up like bananas hanging on a hook.

To reach Dima's newly established high point, Jula and I had to ascend the rope he had anchored for us. I had to pass through the wet chimney with one of our heavy packs on, a brutal struggle that felt like trying to squeeze a pig through a laundry chute. After an interesting mix of grunting and colorful language, Jula and I each made our way to our anchor and new high point, leaving behind the comfort and safety of the ledge.

Above the stance was what we call an "off-width" crack. This is a size of crack considered too wide to easily jam your finger, hand or fist into and pull on, but smaller than a chimney, where you can slip your body into to make progress. It is the most feared crack size to climb, as it feels extremely insecure, and most often is very difficult to protect against a fall. There are a handful of manufacturers who build devices to protect wider cracks, but they are very heavy. Maybe this is why we had decided to leave this one device, which would have helped, at base camp.

I began to feel regret as I faced my lead through the off-width, but quickly focused with determination and presence.

Remarkably, as soon as I completely committed to the crack by inserting my foot and knee, along with my left arm and shoulder, the difficulty seemed to relent enough for me to quickly make fifteen feet of progress. At this point, I was physically spent. I had more energy and power in reserve, but as these were my first lead moves of the day, the mental effort, and thinner air made the moment feel rather desperate. Weighing heavy on my mind was the fact that having fifteen feet of rope out back to the anchor meant a slip here would result in a fall of more than thirty feet, and most critically, would directly impact the anchor system.

The first moments when you start a new section of climbing are most critical. The leader needs to quickly place a piece of gear to avoid a fall directly onto the anchor or the ground. The first gear placement establishes a point on the wall that the rope will run through, absorbing the forces generated by a fall instead of all the impact force hitting the belayer and anchor system. By committing and cranking out the first fifteen feet, I'd been able to find a perfect foothold outside the crack at precisely the point where I was starting to most anxiously feel the need to get a piece of gear in. I carefully placed my sticky rubber climbing shoe onto the hold and balanced with my face pressed against the granite to gain the relief and support it offered.

Refocusing on my labored breathing, I managed to reel in my racing heartbeat and clear my head so I could focus on finding a good gear placement. Above me, the crack narrowed just enough to accept my largest piece of gear. While my hand clung to a small edge inside the crack, I slid the gear into the crack with one hand. I then pulled up the rope, clenched it in my teeth, and pulled up another arm's length of rope so I could reach above and clip it into the gear I had placed. I struggled, my foot starting to shake on the single foothold that was keeping me pasted to the sheer face.

Falling while clipping with so much rope out is a big no-no; the air-time before impact is much higher. With extreme focus, I clipped the rope and announced to Dima and Jula that I was now protected. They were relieved as much as I was and cheered me on. I think Dima may have even smiled, but I'll never know for sure. I looked up at the seemingly endless wall above. It was still incredibly intimidating, but for the first time on the climb, the sheer beauty of the line affected me. Just that moment, the sun came out. I took a deep breath trying to absorb it all, and for a fleeting moment, I felt joy; the joy of climbing. "Yes! Air, Vertical; I am connected…this is why I climb!" Those fleeting moments fuel your forward momentum.

 The line is a term used to refer to the path of a specific climbing route.

Above, the crack narrowed to a much more enjoyable size, ranging from the width of your fist to the thickness of your hand. This allowed me to start moving with more confidence. I had gear that fit the crack and placed a piece every fifteen to twenty-five feet. I would have liked to have placed more, but we had to conserve gear to ensure we would have enough to build a solid anchor at the end of each section of climbing. As mentioned earlier, when building anchors, we use three to four pieces of gear for redundancy and strength. Add the fact that three to four pieces make up the anchor below, and this only leaves about fifteen pieces for the leader to use. In addition, not all of the pieces will fit, so you end up with between five and ten pieces of gear to place in a 150-

200-foot section of climbing. You hope that what you have left over for the anchor will be what you need.

I paid close attention to my gear selection, trying to look ahead to anticipate what I might need for the anchor as I balanced my options and placed pieces on the way up. I pushed on for more than 190 feet and was forced to decide on an anchor location as I was about to run out of rope.

While I had high hopes for a place to stand at the end of my lead, the wall was steep and devoid of resting spots. We would have to hang directly on the gear, our feet swinging in the air. I set up a solid anchor with three redundant pieces of gear, each capable of holding more than 5000 pounds of force—roughly triple the impact load in an average fall. Despite the lack of a ledge to stand on, my spirit was lifted by the beautiful crack that stretched above us, and the sun was out.

Having a clear path ahead and a good weather window gave us the momentum we needed to cover some good ground in the afternoon of Day Two. Throughout the day, we faced steeper– angled rock. The crux above our ledge had us careening backward to read the route above as the angle went beyond vertical. After my lead, Dima took the next lead and made good time to the next anchor. Our speed bottleneck at this point was getting Jula and me up the rope efficiently. Ascending the steep lines was absolutely miserable. The heavy backpacks made every movement a grind; it felt like ten people were hanging on our arms and back trying to drag us back to earth.

Dima climbing on the morning of Day Two, fully committed to the northwest pillar

Dima building momentum, Mid-Day Two

Dima ascending high on the Central Pyramid on Day Two

After Dima's pitch, he offered to take the lead again, but I said no thanks. I was happy to grab the end of the rope and looking forward to beautiful climbing. The mental engagement required to be on lead was a small burden relative to the horrendous physical grind of moving the gear up. I arranged the gear, took a few sips of water and got ready to lead. I was hungry already, but we were nowhere near a good place to prepare food. We all dug deeper, grasping for the strength to keep climbing, and I launched myself up into The Vertical again.

This section of climbing went well, but the difficulty increased as we neared the 2000-foot mark on the wall. The elevation was around 12,000 feet above sea level. While the oxygen was getting thinner, I think we had more oxygen than food, and less water than either. I was concerned that we were critically low on water and it appeared that we would be nowhere near the summit before sunset. On top of that, we weren't even sure that we'd find water on the summit; that was an Andre idea, after all. The supply situation was even more reason to move as quickly as possible, but we started to lose the balancing act between energy expended and fuel consumption, and our pace slowed.

It was Dima's turn to lead again as the sun began to set. Had we anywhere to sleep, the sensible decision would have been to set up camp and prepare dinner in the daylight, but we were still floating on a sea of sheer granite. Dima pushed on as dusk fell, with Jula and I reaching his anchor station inside the base of a dark chimney. The moment the sun disappeared completely and the last rays of sunlight moved on to light some other stretch of the planet, a strong, cold wind began to blow directly down the wall. This would have been the most miserable place to hang and try to rest.

Dima laboring with one of our heavy packs on exposed steep terrain late on Day Two

I was starting to freak out again as the reality of our commitment and exposure were screaming out to us.

We were way too far up the wall to go down. The weather was clearly making a turn for the worse. We had no ledge to sleep on, and both our food and water supplies were desperately low. I was frozen in the chaos of our self-inflicted struggle.

Fortunately, Dima carried enough courage for all of us. I remember him looking us in the eyes as we all huddled together. "Manley, Jula—maybe I lead rope again, up, find ledge." Before he could change his mind, I started setting up my belay for him and threw him the sharp end, or leading end, of the rope. "Take it, Dima! I'll stay here and keep your wife warm."

He cracked the slightest grin possible. Finally. This was a rare moment for Dima. For nearly every second of the journey, his stoic face had shielded joy from the rest of the world. It added a seriousness to an already intense situation. Jula's demeanor was much easier to enjoy. Reassuring, she created a good buffer between Dima's iron-heart approach and my strategy of fueling the party with positive energy and smiles.

Dima cast off into the raging wind, which was now funneling down the chimney at what felt like thirty miles per hour. Jula and I huddled together, shivering in the darkness. I prayed. This was a time in my life in which I wasn't praying or attending any traditional church, so it felt rather hypocritical at first. But, when you are pressed into the darkest corners of fear in your life, I've found you will call out for the best of any beliefs you've ever been exposed to. The voice of fear, which had been present for a full year leading up to the trip, was even louder now, and doubt flooded my mind. At certain moments in the trip, the feeling that death was waiting for me on this journey grew much stronger and vividly present. At these moments, I had focused inwardly, on my desire to accomplish a climb in this beautiful mountain range, and I looked upward to the summit. That action, which helped refocus my energy towards progress, encouraged my partners, and even my Italian friends on the ground before the climb started. This moment was no different. I prayed for strength and reached deep inside my soul for more courage, and yelled up to Dima, "you rock Dima! Climb on, my friend, I have you on belay!" I'm not sure how much he actually understood the words, but the tone of my voice and unwavering enthusiasm in my message was clear. It would often draw a simple, loud and powerful response from Dima: "Da Manley, da! Summit!"

When Dima was in sight, I could see my words of encouragement lift his physical energy, as he would stretch a bit higher and spring forth with fire. In the darkness of our cold granite shaft, the rope inched upward. But occasionally, it would make a steadier surge—our only sign Dima had not given up and was continuing the battle above. An hour and twenty minutes felt like five hours had passed before Dima's voice was able to find its way down the wall between blasts of wind. "I found ledge! Manley, Jula, I have ledge!" he shouted with more enthusiasm than I had heard him express in the entire trip so far. My emotional response went way beyond relieved to ecstatic. My mind raced to imagine the comfort of this wonderful ledge Dima had labored to secure for our rest. But then I thought, wait a second—I'd better not get too excited.

"Dima!" I shouted. "Is the ledge good?"

"*It's as good as gold*, Manley!" His words rang out across the wall and echoed in my mind. I didn't just go there mentally, I fully checked in. Imagine the most beautiful hotel suite you've ever seen in your life. I was there. My legs kicked up on the leather sofa. I stretched. Dima and Jula rubbed my tired feet and brought me tea. Oh, man, was it a good fantasy. Too bad it didn't last much beyond that mental mirage.

Do you think the ledge was really that good?

I left our miserable anchor station first and went to battle in the chimney, cleaning the gear Dima had placed to protect his daring nighttime grind up the chasm.

Cleaning the gear is the task of the climber who climbs up after the leader has established the anchor system, often referred to as the second, as in the second person up. The process can be very demanding, as some pieces of gear can be difficult to extract from the wall. The second is very motivated to clean all of the gear that was placed by the lead climber; gear is expensive, and most importantly, leaving a piece behind could prove to be an epic mistake should that piece of gear be the exact one you need later for safety or escape from the wall.

Jula was able to take a line up the second rope out on the face, but was struggling to move with the supply pack weighing her down. It took us nearly an hour to make our way up the strenuous 175 feet to reach Dima.

The ledge was *"good as gold,"* all right. (It sucked!) It was smaller than a picnic table, three feet across and five feet long, covered with viciously sharp loose rocks ranging from little golf balls to softball-sized. Now tilt the ledge 30 degrees into the void. Welcome to "good-as-gold" ledge.

By the time we secured our packs and I inspected the anchor, we started setting up their tent. The wind was now blasting at over forty miles per hour and made everything extremely challenging. When the strongest gust came, we would all pile on top of each other, one hand grasping at anything on the closest body we could hold onto, the other hand gripping the tent as tightly as possible. It took us more than thirty minutes to erect the tent and crudely secure it to the wall—a job that usually took five. The wind alternated between intense downward gales that would flatten the tent and random upward gusts that would pick up the tent, twisting and tearing it. The only way we could lessen the damage was to crawl inside and act as living weights to anchor it down.

Imagine taking the honeymoon suite on the inside where Dima and Jula had crawled. By the time I slid into the remaining space, more than half my body hung over the sloping edge, my legs from the knees down flapping in the wind.

Just as I had come to grips with our evening ahead, Dima announced the craziest idea I had ever heard in all my days in The Vertical. "Manley, need hot water for tea!"

"What? There's no way! We'll catch the tent on fire. And even if we were able to boil water safely, we should use the water to eat our last freeze-dried meal." We tried to have a conversation about rations, fire safety, and the meaning of life. I tried to convince them it was a ridiculous idea to try and burn our jet-fuel stove inside the tent. They insisted. Dima and Jula *insisted* on trying to get the stove going, explaining, "body need food, tea for summit."

I don't know why I went along with the half-cocked idea; perhaps hunger overcame my better judgment.

Dima held the tent up and Jula took a position towards the back corner of the ledge to anchor the tent down at a point where the wind was building momentum and attempting to roll all of us off the ledge. I took a precarious position sitting up, and with several nylon supply bags as padding on top of my legs and sleeping bag, I created a small crater that enabled me to hold the base of the stove steady with my right hand. With my left hand, I used a pot grabber, a pliers-like tool, to precariously grip the edge of the handle-less two-quart pan.

Getting the dirty jet-fueled stove to fire up and come to life was easy. Holding the two-quart pot stable while making sure the flames of the stove didn't leap onto anything else drained my aching body of my last energy. With merely three thin metal edges on the burner of the stove to support the pan, it wanted to slide off with the slightest shift. At base camp, it took more than ten minutes to boil water. With the added elevation, and in the awful position I was cramping up in, it seemed like an hour. Finally, we had two quarts near boiling—the perfect amount for two freeze-dried meals.

The only thing more shocking than Dima's insistence that we fire up my jet fuel stove was that he and Jula wanted to use the hot water to drink tea. I encouraged them to use it for our food, but they were adamant. Then they discovered that we were out of tea. "Actually, this is good," I thought. "I won't need to convince them to eat now." Not so fast. They chose to drink the hot water with no tea—nothing. Very odd indeed. "Y'all can drink a quart of hot water if you want, but I'm using my quart to make dinner!" I insisted.

After I ate my dinner and they were recharged by their hot water, we all became more confident in my act of fire-balancing. We decided to boil two more quarts so they could also have dinner. That was the good news. As we rummaged through the bottom of our food bag, we realized that we had only one dinner left, and just enough water to cook our final meal. "We are completely out of food and water!" I announced to Dima and Jula.

"No more water, Manley? No more food?" We all stared at each other for several minutes. Finally, Dima broke the silence, "Summit, Manley. Summit maybe ice, maybe water."

I responded with delirious optimism, "Yes! Summit! Tomorrow we summit, then back to base camp for celebration! We will eat big with our friends!" It was a distraction, but effective. We all smiled at each other, haggard, but reassured that we would make it to the summit and down to eat and drink merrily once again.

The night passed in a few hours, but dragged on for days in our minds. We took turns holding the tent off our faces so we wouldn't suffocate in our sleep while the others tried to sleep in the deafening roar of the wind. Dragging myself out of our battered shelter and getting ready to climb was the most difficult morning of my life. Our bodies ached and begged for mercy; our mouths were dry from the altitude and night of shallow breathing in the wind storm. By the time the full morning light lit up the south-facing walls behind us, the raging gale had declined to a breeze. The wind diminished, but colder temperatures had settled in, adding misery to our existence on the shadowed north face.

I remember looking down at that ledge and taking this photo.

Dima on "Good-as-Gold Ledge," the cold morning of Day Three

"Good as gold ledge."

I had a realization that morning that has served me well in all aspects of my life.

When you ask the right questions, you get the results you expect.

Vertical Momentum: From Insight to Action

"The highest form of Human Excellence is to question oneself and others." *Socrates*

Clearly, my asking "is the ledge good," was the wrong question. Now, many years later, I laugh at that question. Better questions are often obvious in hindsight.

What should I have asked to more accurately set my expectations and realize the results I expected?

"How big is the ledge? Is it level? Does it have a sofa on it?"

I have learned that when you ask clear, specific questions, better results follow.

I've also noticed that:

- Better service and support people ask better questions.

- Better salespeople ask better questions.

- Better parents ask better questions.

- Better friends ask better questions.

In addition to asking more specific questions about the ledge, I see that I asked a *closed* question—a question that can be answered with a single word or short phrase. An *open* question, one likely to result in a long answer, could have created the space for Dima to describe the ledge in more detail. An example could be, "Can you describe the ledge to me Dima?"

Perhaps he would have still responded "It's as good as gold!" That's when you can use a powerful two-word question that can drive the conversation deeper or expand the focus: "What else?"

To dive deeper into beliefs and drivers for behaviors, we can ask, "Why?" This is how I should have addressed the locking carabiner issue earlier on the climb. In that case, I didn't even ask a question at all; I just told them and showed them what I wanted. The right question at the right time can be the most efficient path to the results you want.

Here are a few powerful questions that can help drive performance:

- "Is this the best we can do?"

"What are we struggling with?"

 "What is getting in the way of us taking this to the next level?"

I also love questions that help focus on the positive aspects of what *is* going well, so you can amplify positive results and behavior. Asking the following questions on a consistent basis can help build momentum and morale:

 "What is working well?"

 "Where are we succeeding?"

The right questions can also create a powerful framework to reflect, debrief, and build momentum after any effort. Try asking one question to focus on the positive aspects of the experience, then a question to help uncover the opportunities to improve next time. I have used the following two-question framework to effectively evaluate and constantly improve myself, as well as the efforts and results of my teams and clients over the years.

 What did you *like best*?

 Next time, what would improve the results?

Here is a simple way to start improving your questions. Intentionally carve out a few minutes as you prepare for your next interaction or meeting and brainstorm, asking yourself, what is one question I want to ask that could be most helpful? Write a few possible questions down and try them. The more you start to be strategic and intentional with your questions, the faster you'll start realizing the results you want.

If you will commit to constantly driving awareness and improving your questioning skills, you will consistently be rewarded.

My key question for you is:

Are you asking the right questions to drive the right results?

Additionally, what one question, if you asked it consistently every day of your life, could change everything for you? Ask, reflect, take action, and reap the rewards of a life lived with more intention.

CHAPTER 8

Vertical Lesson 6: Anchor Your Actions

Early on that cold morning of Day Three living on the wall, July 2, 1999, I took the first lead off Good-as-Gold Ledge. To call my pace turtle-like would be unfair to a species that has been picked on a lot. "An unbearably slow and cold grind" would be the best description. The wall was the coldest I had experienced on the trip so far, completely shaded by its north exposure; it would be late afternoon, at the earliest, if we would see any sunlight at all. The climbing was in my face, the exposure dizzying. While my brain and emotional response system acclimated to the exposure, there were moments of clarity during my lead when the sky below seemed to open up around my feet. It felt like someone had turned up the gravity by a factor of ten.

The wall was dead vertical, featureless except for two cracks that formed massive loose blocks shaped like antique caskets between them. I danced carefully around them making only three moves to advance ten to twelve feet at a time, before my hands and arms would cramp and my fingertips would go numb. I would place a piece of gear in the rock and have Dima pull the rope tight so I could hang on the gear. This allowed me to put my freezing hands in my pants until I could feel them again.

Making the transition from trusting your own hands and feet for upward progress to hanging on your rope and gear can be abrupt and unnerving. One moment you are fully in control and have constant biofeedback used to build mental momentum. The next moment, you are having to rebuild trust in equipment that is intended to only catch you should you screw up and fall. Equally stressful is the moment when you have to commit to your trust in your partner's belay. Traditionally, overcommunicating at this transition helps the lead climber become comfortable enough to depend on the system. It often goes like this:

> **Lead climber:** "Hey—you got me? You got me on belay? I'm sketching up here!"
>
> **Belayer:** "I got you, man! I've got you on belay! Go for it!"
>
> **Lead climber:** "I need you to take rope in. I've gotta hang on this gear or I'm gonna fly." Or in truly desperate moments, the one-word version is: "*take!*"

As quickly as possible, your belayer reels in as much rope as possible to minimize the distance of your fall and enables you to mentally and physically recover.

Of course, when you are limited to a fifty-word vocabulary and have mountain wind and rock between you and your partner, overcommunicating is tricky, if not impossible. Any and all communication was a struggle from the time Dima and I had shaken hands in the valley below. Add some challenging environmental variables and you can forget relying on communicating with your partner to help you feel confident about anything. (As mentioned earlier, reassurance and constant communication between the lead climber and belayer is a secret to momentum and consistently stretching your comfort zone during your ascent. Should you need to trust your belayer and gear more directly, as I had to do for the first hundred feet of my lead that morning—it is ruthless test of courage.)

After making the transition from free climbing to directly trusting the system multiple times, it became easier. I've noticed that about even small acts of courage; they can build big-time momentum. Even if the courage you are building is in the act of temporarily surrendering to the effort, as long as you *work to master the art of the restart*, you will build more momentum than you lose and develop more courage to climb on.

Master the Restart

After one hour and one hundred feet of struggle, my commitment to the grind paid off. I was warmed up, my mind was locked in, and I was able to tap my well of courage. I unleashed my momentum on the last eighty feet of vertical. Man, that felt good. The struggle was still there, but with consistent *restarts* and just a few clicks down on the dial of variables pushing me near my edge, I finally felt like I was getting somewhere, albeit very slowly. Up to now, it was as if I had been driving with the brakes on in first gear. At this point, I let off the brakes, but still couldn't get out of first gear. It turns out, sometimes first gear is all you have, and all you need.

Slowly and steadily, grinding but gaining, first gear worked and got me to the end of my rope. I set up our anchor and belayed up Jula and Dima. Dima's next lead went faster and he was able to push us well above the 2000-foot level on the wall to a completely hanging anchor in The Vertical, floating in a sea of white granite.

Faster than I was ready, it was once again time for me to take the rope into the unknown above.

Dima leading intimidating and cold in-your-face rock on the morning of Day Three

Next we pulled out our pitiful hand-drawn topo map and tried to pretend that it affirmed we were near the summit. Were we really going to reach the summit soon? Where exactly on the face were we? What if we got off route and encountered a dead-end blank section of rock? What was next?

Recover. Reassess. Refuel.

Refuel; ouch. No food, no water. *This sucks!*

That was the salt in the wound for us. Yes, it was cold. Yes, we were not sure we would make the summit on Day Three. Yes, the climbing was pushing our physical capacity for suffering and performance after multiple days of grinding our skin against the cheese-greater like granite. Yes, the altitude slowed our physical abilities and made simple tasks on the wall steal away our breath. Our heads were being assaulted by two sources of headache—one imposed by the thinning air, the other from dehydration. It had now been twelve hours since the last drops of liquid had hit our tongues, and our brains were burning. Our stomachs were scorched with stomach acid, radiating and merging with wrenching lower-back pain from hanging in our harnesses for days.

Living in your harness for more than a few hours can be very uncomfortable. After one full day, I typically have bruised ribs and sores on my hips. This climb truly tortured my midsection; an open wound had formed on my hip bone early on Day Two. For the rest of the climb, with every movement, my harness would grind a deeper groove into my flesh. By the afternoon of Day Three, it had grown into a bloody and pus-infected mess and had enlarged to an inch-and-a-half tall by three-and-a-half inches wide. The reminder still shines today as scarred skin. One plus was the fact that when I was climbing on lead, my movements were more varied, and my harness inflicted a lesser degree of pain than when I was cleaning gear or helping haul our equipment. This helped motivate me to get fired up about being on the sharp end again.

With no refueling or nourishment to be had, I was able to leverage only one minor advantage for my next lead. I climbed as high as possible up onto the anchor that Dima had built and clipped directly into the uppermost piece of gear, a yellow #2 Metollius caming unit.

A **caming unit** is a retractable, reusable metal device that the lead climber places to protect against a fall, or in this case, to anchor the team to the wall. When placed properly in solid rock this equipment can withstand massive weight and impact—an essential element to climbing safely.

Jula's and Dima's heads were at my feet, and they worked to hand me the last pieces of gear leftover from Dima's lead. The eerie silence and solitude of our position gave me a moment of brief clarity to focus and dig deeper into my soul's reserves. That moment of peace was quickly destroyed by an exploding *pop* and the sickening sound of metal grinding against rock. Instantly I was launched into the air and felt myself rocketing towards the ground below. I then slammed with a riveting force directly on the remaining pieces of the anchor in a jolt that shocked my entire being.

My head was now below Dima and Jula's feet, with all three of us and all of our gear swinging wildly in the void. There were more than 2,000 feet of air below, and gravity ruthlessly grasped at our feet, our lives dangling in the balance. One of the three gear placements in our anchor had failed. Typically, when anchors fail, people die. Especially in the high-impact scenario our accident created, a five foot strap I used to connect to the anchor, called a daisy-chain, has no dynamic ability to absorb critical impact forces that the climbing rope would typically handle. What might appear to be a safe and short ten-foot fall right at the anchor is the falling and anchor-failure scenario most climbers have learned to avoid at all costs.

I'm not going to tell you what I said next.

I can tell you this: it was the most colorful display of Kentucky English you can possibly imagine. It would have made the Devil repent and blush before the first sentence was out of my mouth. I went *off* on Dima, because his anchor had nearly killed us, and it was due to a simple error in executing the basics of building anchors.

I could teach you the basics and how to avoid the critical mistake Dima had made when he built an anchor in fewer than five minutes. I know he had the knowledge and skills to execute. I believe he just happened to overlook a critical detail; how well all sides of the device were engaged in the rock. He failed to evaluate the details of his placement, and then I happened to hang directly on the device in a way that exposed its weakness in that moment.

Unfortunately, in that moment, all of my fears and frustrations from the entire adventure erupted in my partners' faces. After I let Dima and Jula know how I really felt about their safety systems and lack of focus on the basics, I rebuilt the anchor to my standards. First, I added two pieces of gear that were each capable of supporting us, and then I improved the two he had placed, and additionally equalized all four pieces so that any impact would be spread dynamically across all the gear. Establishing an anchor I could trust was absolutely essential before I could climb into the unknown again.

I'm not sure why we all survived that moment. Perhaps one reason is so I could share this experience with you now on these pages.

The three Metolius cams from our anchor. After the middle cam pulled, only the units on the left and right kept us barely attached to the wall.

Vertical Momentum: From Insight to Action

DON'T BLOW THE BASICS

Dima blew the basics. In The Vertical, fortunately I've only blown the basics three times, and fortunately in all three situations, I caught my own lack of execution before any consequences were realized.

In my day-to-day life, I've blown the basics countless times; most often it went unnoticed. This is dangerous and breeds complacency. Simple choices, small details, seem inconsequential in the moment. Ultimately, it can all catch up with you.

We all need anchors in our life. I've found that we don't always have them, and in a sense, they may even be optional. Just as true growth is optional, we are in control; we can stay where we are and not leverage tools to give us the confidence to move forward. When we establish points in our lives we can count on—something to fall back on, a worst-case plan, illustrated in enough detail that at least in our minds we know it is *possible*, new expanses open before us. In a new moment of clarity, we are able to see through the fear that can blind us and see opportunities we couldn't see before; or maybe we can see just far enough ahead to make the next move.

The anchor is a critical component in the art of Vertical passage and will serve you in reaching more of your potential in life as well. When people I've worked with have clarity around what protects them from absolute failure and destitution, they are able to move forward carefully and courageously. We need to know that if we fall, our belayer will lock off the rope and stop our fall. We need to know if a piece of gear we have placed on our lead along the way fails, the *next* one will stop us. And ultimately, we must be able to count on that anchor. We must know that no matter what, our anchor is going to hold up and keep the entire team from getting blown off the mountain.

"No power so effectually robs the mind of all its powers of acting and reasoning as fear." Edmund Burke

ANCHOR YOUR ACTIONS

The *Anchor Your Actions* strategy is the most powerful technique I have uncovered to help you expand and climb out of your comfort zone. It has been the secret to overcoming the most terrifying moments of my life in The Vertical, business, and personal arenas. Without fail, every time, it has helped me find the courage to climb into the unknown.

This powerful tool came into my life in 2011. I was facing one of the most difficult decisions I would ever make—one that put my family in jeopardy of bankruptcy, introduced an enormous amount of stress, and exposed us to risk that I had worked hard for fifteen years to remove from our lives. I remember having what seemed like everything I *logically* needed in place to make a sound decision, yet fear of the unknown kept me from making the final commitment. I vacillated between options, called on friends and family for insight, and lost days and days of sleep over the decision.

I ran my dilemma by a close friend and climbing partner. After listening to my struggle and reasoning, on both sides of the options, he asked, "What's your anchor look like?"

"Huh?" I responded, "what do you mean, my anchor?"

"You know, your anchor. Worst case, what will you do if you go for this option and it doesn't work? What would you do?"

So I responded. He pressed for more details.

And then, the breakthrough technique was born. He asked me to *write it down in great detail.*

I pushed back: "I just told you what I would do, who I would call first, the next step, and so on. Everything I would do to recover and restart should my crazy idea not work. Why should I write it down?"

"Just do it. Trust me. Every detail, every step; write it all down and get it out of your head."

When you put the pen to paper, fear separates from fact.

I don't think either of us knew how powerful that key step would be. Reluctantly, that same day I carved out the time and put the pen to paper. The more I wrote, the more I slowly felt the stress of the unknown lose its power over me. We are such emotional creatures. Ideas that exist only in our heads can drown us in a sea of emotion; it's a wonder any of them make it to see the light of reality. When we get ideas out of our heads, emotion falls aside. I wrote nearly two pages, detailing every tactical and strategic step of my contingency plan, and then I read it back. On paper, only the facts remained and I was able to more accurately evaluate the practicality of my anchor. It was all reasonable, every step doable. The more I read it, the more I realized, *I can do this!*

Whatever you do, don't skip actually *writing* out your worst-case anchor plan. The magic is in getting it out of your head. When I've had people do this exercise in a workshop or coaching session and they read it back, they are most often empowered to move forward. Even if they decide to not move forward, they usually feel liberated, knowing they have more fully explored what is possible outside the influence of their emotions.

Know that this exercise can be used for small acts of courage as well, such as asking an uncomfortable question in a meeting or having a conversation you've been avoiding.

How to Leverage the *Anchor Your Actions*: Exercise

Create a space in your day where you can focus in silence, without distraction, for ten to twenty minutes. Ideally, use a pen and paper, but typing will work as well. Start by writing down the summit you are trying to reach. Take a few minutes to describe in detail what it will look and feel like. The more details you write, the more power your vision will have.

Next, write down in detail your *worst-case scenario.* If you fail to reach your summit, what happens? And then what happens? What next? How does this feel? Write out every last detail, taking the time to note the specific actions you will take upon any failure or setback of each individual component in your system.

My next summit is:

_____

_____

When I reach the summit, I imagine the following

view, feeling, and new perspective:

_____

_____

From my next summit, I will probably be able to see

the following possibilities and next summits:

_____

_____

If I fall, I can count on the following anchors to

protect me from complete failure:

_____

_____

My next steps to recover would be:

_____

_____

Keys to Summit with the Anchor Actions

- Take action and build anchors you trust
- When you put the pen to paper, fear separates from fact
- There's power in the details, and they will propel you forward into the unknown
- As you climb, you must tear down old anchors and rebuild new anchors to move forward
- Remind yourself of your anchor to empower you to follow your fear and focus on your next move

Vertical Inquiries to Build Anchors You Trust and Stretch Your Comfort Zone

- What anchors do you need to build to free you from your fears and empower you to climb out of your comfort zone?
- What anchors need to be broken down to free you to move on and build new ones?

Typically, I evaluate the basic checklist of my anchors three times and then refocus on the next forward action. For the anchor I rebuilt high on the wall in Kyrgyzstan, it took nearly ten times my normal obsessive evaluation and reassuring myself that it would indeed protect us as we pushed on. The same has happened with my scariest decisions and journeys in my day-to-day life. Don't think that just because you've written up your detailed worse case anchor that the fear will be gone forever. Expect and plan to leverage it day-to-day, as needed, when fear creeps up in your head and steals the wind from your sails.

Anchor Your Actions in Accountability

The third insight from the *Anchor Your Actions* lesson is perhaps the most important of all. In April of 2016, I was deep in preparation for a series of thirty conference keynotes I was to deliver for an organization. For days on end, I obsessively examined each of the Vertical Lessons, critically focused on customizing my keynote to ensure each one was as relevant as possible to the specific audience I was serving. It was 2:30 in the morning, and it hit me. All these years, I have been sharing the anchor failure scene with audiences, and passionately expressing how Dima had *Blown the Basics,* nearly killing all of us.

I should have checked the anchor myself!

The realization caused me to sit up in bed, shocked. How could it have taken me nearly two decades to see this insight? I have multiple issues with what happened on the wall that day and my portrayal of the event in the years since, and none of them are focused on Dima. Now I shine the light *on me!* The first problem is that *I failed to be accountable* to the safety of our team by not confirming the quality of the anchor.

Of course, as the technically designated "leader" of that section of climbing, it was Dima's primary responsibility, and he should have built a better anchor. For critical components of the climbing system, we are all accountable. If I had examined the anchor when I arrived, I would have noticed Dima's mistake and proactively corrected it before it put our lives in grave danger.

When you consistently anchor your actions through the lens of your accountabilities to others, you step up to lead at a higher level.

Secondly, *great leaders look inward first.* I cut myself some slack for losing my cool in that extraordinarily stressful moment, but to continue to point the finger outward at my teammate for all these years is a leadership failure. *Before you point the finger at someone else, you'd better check yourself.* Great leaders, regardless of title, courageously step up in many ways.

CHAPTER 9:

Vertical Lesson 7: Celebrate The Summits!

Moments before sunset, on July 22nd, I took the last lead, stretched out my red rope, and crawled onto the summit. To the east I could see towards Tibet and China. Behind me, walls reached to the sky above with peaks stretching south into Afghanistan. To the west there were mountains for as far as I could see—mountains that have yet to be named and yet to be climbed. I was physically, mentally, and emotionally absolutely wasted. But, as the team reached the summit with me, our lives were lit with our smiles, even Dima. We were relieved, elated, and *anxious*.

Summits in the big hills brings both joy and dread. Yes, there often is a positive, euphoric, emotional moment, but most often the physical and mental exhaustion temper what you might imagine as a block party in the sky. Compounded with physical and emotional energy tanks being empty, a serious pit usually forms in the stomach when the unavoidable question hits: *How are we going to get down?*

Sure, you have a strategy before you ever start. But as anyone who's ever completed a project of any magnitude will tell you, variables shift constantly, and the course of your adventure always has surprises in store. In our case, we still had some pressing,

Dima on the summit of the Central Pyramid

urgent issues. We were still out of food and water. That evening marked 24 hours without a drop of water intake. Had the weather been hot, this would have been more than just suffering. In the colder weather on Day Three of living on the wall, we found the cold temperatures to be a silver lining.

I'll never forget how it felt when the sun set that evening. I was exhausted. I was hungry. I was still scared. I was also filled with a sense of intense joy. I was grateful with the absolute certainty that while I may not have had the perfect climbing partners, there was no way I would have made it there without them. They weren't perfect partners, but they were *incredible* partners.

We spent the third night on a pile of rocks, balanced on the ethereal summit of the Central Pyramid, Aksu 3850. The tent was near collapsing, and after struggling to sleep cramped up next to Dima and Jula, I crawled out around 2:00 a.m. This was an absolutely surreal moment. The moon lit the summit, the

Dima belaying Jula to the summit of the Central Pyramid, with the Russian Tower behind him

Dima at sunset on the majestic summit of the Central Pyramid

surrounding peaks, and the endless walls of shimmering granite faces. Grateful. For the first time of the expedition, and as much as any moment in my life, I felt absolute peace. I felt like I was on the moon. For a few hours of that magical night, I transcended the boundaries of my normal existence. I was intensely present and alive in every single cell of my being. I was detached from my life, but fully aware and completely connected to everything in the universe. Yes. The summit, then sleep.

Jula and I on the summit of the Central Pyramid, on the morning of Day Four on the wall

Vertical Momentum: From Insight to Action
CELEBRATE ALL SUMMITS, BIG AND SMALL

I believe we "summit" more often than we realize in our lives. Some days, it's all a grind. The climbing never stops, or perhaps despite our best efforts and all the energy we have already invested, conditions erode our spirit and we feel like we have made zero progress. Our course could also take on a traverse or even lose ground instead of rebuilding our forward momentum.

I'm not in favor of a false or inflated view of circumstances. Do you feel like you celebrate your summits enough? Big and small? I've asked this question of audience members around the world and the unified answer is "No."

We all need to celebrate the summits more often, and we don't have to wait for a big one; the little ones count, too. We also don't need to have any certain title or position to celebrate the summits. *Do not wait for permission.* Start now, even if you're the only one dancing on top! Most people I work with say even the big summits are rarely celebrated in the way they should be, and certainly, most small summits—those little day-to-day victories—are almost always overlooked. It is not easy to consistently celebrate our summits, but when we do, the payoff is huge. The payoff is momentum.

Celebrating Summits Builds Momentum

Great clarity can be gained from your next summit. Through the lens of success on your next summit, your view will be enhanced with optimism and expanded perspective. Do not miss this incredible opportunity to *redefine what is possible.*

Celebrate big, but briefly: In the mountains, we always celebrate the summit, but we move on quickly. If we hang out for too long on the summit, a storm can come, or lighting can strike you down, or at the very least, the sun sets making your descent to safety more dangerous than it needs to be.

I've learned to do the same in business and life. Have you had a moment in your life where you have hit your summit—perhaps a project finished successfully—and then you celebrate, and relax, assuming everything is good? Then, seemingly out of nowhere, you get slammed with a storm; maybe news that the project is now having problems. This has happened to me with several business projects. The project goes live, or we believe the effort is complete, so we celebrate, but for too long. We hang out at the top, perhaps even dropping our guard or becoming complacent in the sunshine of the summit. Then we get hit with a reality check, discovering that the work is not done or that there are issue that needs our attention.

Perspective is Power: Take note of potential next summits that come into view. Look around. You will see opportunities you can't see from where you are today when you reach your next summit—opportunities you can't even imagine from the safety of your base camp, nor during the struggle of the climb. Ask your team, *what should we climb next? Now that we've achieved this, what do you think is possible?* You can point out the next summit opportunities for them, but you might be met with, "Oh boy, now they want us to do *more!*" When they help identify the next summits, the momentum is initialized by them.

Call Back to Your Last Summit in Your Next Struggle: Save your summits, big and small in a journal or other archives, and then review them in your next struggle.

This has worked for me in a variety of life scenarios. What I've discovered is that lessons learned during a previous struggle and summit, even in a completely different part of your life, can provide very powerful ways to help you push through a current struggle. The similarity of the struggle is irrelevant, as long as the struggle and triumph you achieved is an *emotionally significant* part of your climb.

Mini-tripod self-portrait of Jula, Dima, and me on the summit of the Central Pyramid on the morning of Day Four on the wall

I remember swimming in uncertainty when facing an especially difficult decision point in my life.

After my first paid speaking engagement in 1995, my passion and experience for developing people continued to expand while helping grow the revolutionary retail concept, Build-A-Bear Workshop. I moved up the leadership ranks and developed larger teams. We successfully navigated extraordinary business growth, taking our store count from forty to over four hundred worldwide. We weathered the economic storms after September 11, 2001, went public on the New York Stock Exchange, and survived the painful 2008 recession. My ability to grow people and help them reach more of their potential though my Vertical Lessons Keynotes expanded as well, and by the end of the decade, a fire to focus all of my efforts on helping people pushed me to a critical decision point. I saw a former Southwest Airlines trainer, Jason Young, deliver a keynote speech in Miami, and it hit me. I needed to speak for a living. *Now.*

I saw my next summit and started pursuing it with the same fire and drive that had led me though my other storms and summits of life. Only this time, the stakes were higher. I remember the call with my father the afternoon after Jason's keynote. "Dad, I'm changing careers!"

"*What?* You are the sole income provider for your family. It's the worst economy since the 1930's. You work for a great company and have job security, benefits, and you made it to the executive level. Do you want me to go on?" After my Dad's cautionary advice, I surrounded myself with several full-time professional speakers, most of whom encouraged me to *not* quit my day job. However, I quickly came to a point where I could not effectively maintain my responsibilities at Build-A-Bear and grow my impact though my speaking. I knew what my next summit was. I had Incredible Partners lined up, the right tools to use to my advantage, and even a wife who supported all my crazy ambitions. Fear kept cranking emotional gravity up on my head, and even with my heart fully on fire I could not overcome it. I could not pull the final trigger and make the leap into my next Vertical adventure in life.

This created an extraordinary stress internally and affected those closest to me in my life. My incredible wife, Emily, my soulmate, ultimate belayer and love of my life, endured the worst of it. One evening in our home, she ran out of the bedroom, excited. "Honey! Don't you see the signs?"

I was confused, wondering if perhaps she had finally flipped from all the stress I had been inflicting on our family. "Your fear;

that's the sign! What you fear most is exactly what you need to do next. You must go for it! Follow your fear. Climb, damn it!"

"I can't, I'm too scared." I folded into a mess of fear, tears, and anxiety on our couch. That's when her love and brilliance came to the rescue once again.

"Manley, you have done way scarier things in your life. Think about it! You have had so many significant summits, many that pushed you way out of your comfort zone, through fear and to your next summit. What was the most fearful struggle you battled through and succeeded?"

I said "Kyrgyzstan—you know that."

"Tell me about it again; the whole story, all the indecision, when you thought you weren't going to make it. Tell me about when you really wanted to quit, but didn't. I want to hear all the details."

So I did. I told her the story you have just relived with me. God love her, she had heard it all before, but she pressed me to take all the time in the world, and relive it all again with her. When we got to the summit, she asked for more details. Then more introspection into how it *felt* on the summit. Through that process, specifically the detail through which she asked me to relive it, and her focus on the most significant struggles and summit experience, I became supercharged with courage and confidence.

I've used the same technique with myself and coaching clients again and again with startling success.

The next time you are deep in a struggle, or at a fearful point of indecision in life, reach back into your history and relive a previous summit. Again, it does not have to be related to the current struggle. But there are key components. Here are some simple guidelines to help you leverage this technique:

1. Choose a significant struggle in which you eventually succeeded.

2. Write or verbally *relive it.*

3. Relive the emotions of fear and frustration when you were ready to give up.

4. Relive the summit celebration moment.

5. Then commit to one small and low-resistance action toward your next summit.

CHAPTER 10

Vertical Lesson 8: Master the Art of the Restart

The descent is typically the most treacherous and often the most dangerous phase of any mountain-climbing effort. Sometimes the euphoria we might expect is waiting for us on the summit, but more often it is not. It can fail to meet your expectations and leave you empty, or, at the very least, exhausted.

On Day Four, we staggered out of our sleeping bags, starving. Dima woke at sunrise, on a search to soothe our raw, swollen throats from the dry mountain air. More than thirty-six hours had passed since we had had any water, and we were extremely dehydrated. Dima scoured the summit, literally turning over every rock in sight. By the time I crawled out of my sleeping bag, he had found a few softball-sized chunks of ice to melt. After days of struggling, I had finally mastered starting my compact stove with our dirty jet fuel, and we had a strong flame on the ice within three minutes. That was the easy part. Waiting for ice to melt at altitude took a lot of patience, but we were ready to do anything and wait any length of time required to finally get a few sips of water. By the end of our first hour of effort, we each had 2 cups of water and felt refreshed enough to start our descent off the west side of the mountain.

Dima melting ice on the summit, our first water in over a day, the morning of Day Four

Most people assume that the summit is a massive dance party celebration of joy, but as I've described, you are actually exhausted. In addition to that, hanging over your head and heart is the fear of the unknown below, and the reality that more parties are injured or killed getting down from the mountain than climbing to the summit. So, it was with great dread and a sickening feeling in the pit of my stomach that I looked for a path to begin our climb down. On this mountain, like most major objectives, the descent follows a completely different route, which can create another completely epic adventure. There are countless stories of successful summits that were followed by a drastic turn of events, finding climbing parties struggling for their lives as they tried to find their way back to earth on little energy and with dwindling supplies.

This moment was perhaps Dima's most brilliant of all.

Throughout our days in The Vertical, he had demonstrated a solid sense of intuition, helping us choose the most efficient path up the wall at several key crossroads where we could have lost our way. Getting off the top of the Northwest Pillar of the Central Pyramid would prove to be the most critical test of our route-finding ability of the trip. We had some vague directions that our decent should begin directly south of our summit, but ignoring that information, Dima seemed to pull from a strong sense of intuition and asked for my help to explore a different option. "Manley, belay me—I go for descent this way!"

"Huh?" I was confused. Dima pointed into the steep void to the east of our summit, the last place I was comfortable looking for a way down. I got Dima on belay, my red rope piled at my feet and in my hands, stretching across the jagged summit rocks and tied to Dima's filthy harness. His face was as serious and stoic as ever, knowing we were far from the safety of the ground and running on no food. If we picked the right path down, perhaps we would be in base camp by nightfall. But even a few minor mistakes along our descent could find us hanging exposed on the wall, miserably surviving another night out in the mountains.

Off into the void Dima climbed down and traversed, completely out of sight. I could hear rocks falling down the cliff and yelled out, "Dima, are you OK?" On cue, he popped his head above the summit horizon again, a new light in his eyes and a rare smile on his face. "I find way down, Manley!"

His unexpected flash of enthusiasm was all we had to lift our spirits and get moving down the mountain with him.

We traversed seventy feet down and more than 100 feet to our left before we regathered at a small perch the size of a coffee table, hanging in the air more than two thousand feet above a snow- and ice-filled gully. We established an anchor of nylon sling material that we could leave behind and backed it up with our climbing gear for the first two people to descend on. Dima led the entire descent, always going first to find and establish our next anchor station. Jula descended next, followed by me as I broke down the backup anchor, committing to the hand-tied sling anchors we would thread behind rocks and through crack features on the wall. Slings are pieces of webbing, typically hand tied or sewn into a loop. After five anchors and one thousand feet of rappelling our way down through the unknown terrain, we had forged a new path to the base of a snow and ice gully.

Dima felt we should cross the snow and ice gully to another buttress to the east. This seemed like a reasonable idea, except that the snow and ice gully was a gauntlet of falling rocks. We stayed close to the massive wall we had just descended and tried to get a sense of timing for the rockfall. We thought if we could determine a pattern, perhaps we could time a safe crossing. It wasn't constant, yet not a full minute would pass without at least one to three baseball, to football sized rocks flying past. It would only take one to crush your skull, leaving you bleeding to death on the dirty snow and ice.

I pushed back on Dima and his idea. "Too much rock-fall, Dima! I think we need to stay on this wall."

"Manley, no, too steep—look!" Dima pointed below us, and indeed he was right. Our side of the wall appeared to merge back onto overhanging and extremely blank and technical uncharted terrain. And I could see what he was aiming for; the buttress on the other side of the gully looked to be at least half the size of the one we were hanging on. Finally, Dima said, "We go this way. I show you safe."

We set up another rappelling anchor and Dima descended and traversed until he was well within the zone of consistent rock fall. He waited patiently for a little over a minute until the next shower of rock began, taking cover by slamming himself against the ice and snow as the rocks passed. As soon as the group of rocks cleared him, Jula and I yelled "Go, Dima!" and he ran horizontally across the gully, slipping and falling on the snow and ice, but also managing a controlled fall along the rope with his rappelling device. Before the next group of rocks blasted past, he had made it safely through the gauntlet and was at the top edge of the far buttress. Jula went next, her timing as ideal as Dima's, enabling her to reach our next anchor without even having to duck any rock-fall.

I then broke down the backup anchor and started my descent and traverse. I followed our process, waiting until several rocks went past before beginning my vertical dance, traverse and controlled fall across the gauntlet. Just as I ran into the dead center of the gully, I heard Jula and Dima scream, "Rock, Manley! Rock!" I started to look up and saw at least five large rocks blasting down the gully at me while I heard a huge rush of air created by one rock to my left. I slammed my entire body into the snow and ice in front of me just as a concrete-block sized rock jettisoned past my head. As the roar of the rocks flying past increased, I felt like rockets were firing past me. I tightened every muscle in my body and yelled a deep groan of fear and tension from within my soul, bracing for the impact of the remaining rock-fall. It was as though a shield had formed around me. I could see and hear all the rocks bouncing above me, to my left and right, but not a single one even grazed me.

"Run, Manley, *now!*" Dima and Jula gave me the word after the last rock in the series rocketed past. In that moment, the mountain seemed to pause to reload her ammunition, and I scraped, clawed, ran, and rappelled with all the adrenalized energy I've ever experienced across and down the gulley to the small zone of safety they had established for us.

Surviving the rock-fall gauntlet, we started the descent of the buttress below. Our first two rappels went well, taking us four hundred feet down to another small ledge. Up to this point, we had been very lucky while pulling our ropes down. We were able to retrieve them and continue our journey every time without them getting hung up above. And then it happened. Pulling our rope for our next rappel into the void, it got stuck. We tried to flip it, pulled hard, and used every other trick we knew, but the rope wouldn't budge. We were stranded, and left with no choice but to start climbing again. "I will go up and fix it, Dima. You belay me."

Dima set up my belay and I started lead climbing the unknown vertical terrain above. Fortunately, the climbing wasn't too hard, but there was a lot of loose rock. I had to be extremely careful and test every rock I touched so I would not pull one off and threaten the lives of my partners below. Within twenty minutes, I made it to the point where the rope had jammed behind a crack in the wall and was able to free it, then transition back into descent mode. Once again I was reunited with my team, and we continued our journey to the base of the buttress. It took ten 200-foot rappels over 2000 vertical feet and nearly twenty slings left behind to reach a point where we felt comfortable coiling our ropes and putting them on our backs.

Below us remained several thousand feet of terrain to descend at a 45-degree angle. Aside from the extraordinary burn this put on our quadriceps, every few minutes we would slip on the rock. Imagine a 45-degree hill covered in millions of small BB-sized rocks, or scree. It was very slippery, to say the least, especially with the weight on our backs and all of our climbing gear swinging on our sides. But once we got familiar with the odd medium below our feet, we started to gain a rhythm to our semi-controlled slide-and-walk. We further improved our technique by applying a downhill ski technique to the sliding, and then we'd wipe out every few hundred feet. This portion of the descent took nearly two hours, but finally ended with us scrambling past larger boulders to the intersection of the gulley and valley below.

Finally, at around 8:00 p.m., we staggered into the base camp. Our friend Andre and our Italian climbing team friends were filled with joy and celebrated our successful ascent and safe descent back to base camp by treating us to a large meal they had prepared. Looking back I didn't know at the time I would never connect with these people again, but they have been with me on every climb of my life.

I thought getting off the mountain would be the most dangerous part of our journey back home, but little did I know the epic had just begun.

We packed up the donkeys the next morning in just enough time to leave the Aksu Valley on schedule and made our way for two days back to Vorukh, Tajikistan. We spent the evening in Vorukh and then met up with Sultan, our taxi cab driver, and started our long journey back to Bishkek.

Sultan had become a critical support team member on our adventure. Not only did he show up right on schedule weeks

The summit team and Andre upon our safe return to base camp at the end of Day Four

Celebrating my successful climb with the locals back in Vorukh, Tajikistan

later, with no smart phone to remind him, he went out of his way to make our trip home safe and stress-free. Crossing multiple borders and dealing with corrupt, hostile guards in the region was a dreadful experience. Sultan knew the countryside well and navigated hours and hours of single-lane, dirt mountain roads to help us bypass our contrived visits into Uzbekistan and Tajikistan and keep our path primarily within the Kyrgyzstan border. This seemed like a good idea and helped ease my mind. I felt as though I was floating alone in the space of a far mysterious land. Yes, No Problem and Sultan were with me, but taking the trip back without my brother and his assertive and advanced travel skills kept me constantly on edge.

A typical central Asian "restaurant" on our journey back to Bishkek

At first, this strategy worked quite well, as we were able to explore some extremely remote outposts in Uzbekistan, but then Sultan's plan started to fall apart. We pulled up to a small building by the road and Sultan slammed on the brakes as three young men in military uniforms aimed assault rifles at our car and shouted. Simultaneously, two additional men rushed to each side of our car and immediately engaged us with extremely intense faces.

My heart sank and my stomach began to turn over with raw fear. I could tell by their faces this was going to be bad. Sultan's conversation with the apparent leader of the group quickly went from cooperative to a high-intensity argument. His hand gestures and pointing to his map appeared to irritate the group of guards even more. During a brief break in the door-side interrogation of Sultan, he explained that they knew we had missed some other checkpoints and this was going to be "big problem."

"Out, all out, hands up!" Now I was in an absolute panic, but trying to look calm and cool, friendly and cooperative.

"Yes sir, yes sir!" I tried to balance a narrow edge between respect and firm confidence, and when asked, told them, "I am alpinist. I was climbing in Aksu and Kara Su valleys." Cold stares and a massive pit in my stomach. It felt like an hour, but in less than twenty minutes, they ordered us back to their headquarters for "special interrogation and investigate." We were escorted back in a small military convoy to a small town somewhere in central Asia. To this day I have no idea exactly where I was, and I still cannot believe what happened next.

Then No Problem finally called it. "Manfree, maybe problem!"

I felt like I was in a modern day drama spy thriller as the several men came to the car and rudely yelled out to our driver, "Exit! Exit!"

Sultan was taken inside while Misha and I were constantly surrounded by armed guards as we swam in the hopeless anxiety of the moment, temporary prisoners of our car. After forty-five minutes, they ordered Misha and me out of the car and proceeded to split all three of us up. We had no idea what had happened to Sultan, and now I was being escorted away from Misha as they took him toward a third building. What unfolded next was the scariest moment of my life, and to this day feels like a bad dream—an absolutely surreal brush with fate.

A towering man, six-and-a-half feet tall, in a black leather coat, with black hair and ice blue eyes, approached me, showing his badge as he said, "Uzbekistan KGB, walk with me now." He was calm and intense, calculated, and had the most powerful and unnerving presence. The previous guards had gained their influence through outward hostility and intense language; this man's control was much deeper and disturbing. Sensing my panic, he said, "don't worry, my friend, we are just going on a little walk. We need to talk."

I went from anxious to imagining spending the rest of my life hidden away in a dark prison cell in central Asia. He walked beside me, leading me more than two blocks to an old five-story building. We walked up wide limestone steps into the dark building; then he began a slow walk up several flights of stairs. The building seemed vacated, with no electricity, yet it seemed recently maintained. As we arrived at each landing in the staircase, he would pause and look at me, as to say, "no, we are going deeper into this fearful place. You are going far away." We stopped at the fifth floor. I remember looking to the left down the hallway. It was completely dark except for this light gleaming through the window and onto the floor in front of the windows. He said, "Come with me, Manley."

We took this long, slow, quiet walk down to the end of the hallway where he leaned against the windowsill. His blue eyes lit up like crystals in the sunlight that was piercing through the window. His voice seemed to slow and gain an even deeper, more resonant and powerful tone. "Why are you here, Manley?"

"I am a climber, *alpinisto*. We climbed near the Tajikistan and Kyrgyzstan border." He continued to interrogate me and asked me more details about my trip, what climb I had done, where I was from, where did I live, and most pointedly, why were we taking the route we were traveling back to Bishkek. Of course, I had no idea, which made telling a consistent story easy. I told him I had hired the driver, I had no idea where we were going, and that we were trying to get back to Bishkek.

At first I'm not sure he believed me, or perhaps it was just standard interrogation techniques behind the iron curtain. He questioned me again and again, probing for lies or inconsistencies in my story. Everything I told him was true. I heard my Dad's voice ringing out in my head: "Son, when you tell the truth, it's easy to remember what you told someone." This frustrated the tall man, especially the consistent answer to the same question, "Why are you here, now?"

Again and again, I replied the same. "I am an *alpinisto*, here to climb in these amazing mountains. That's it." *Alpinisto* was a good label, it turns out, as I had been given direction on this by No Problem early in the trip. During all previous harassment by authorities, this seemed to help us exit the situation quickly, but this time was different. The stakes were higher, the isolation magnified; separation from my driver, guard, and being days from my brother spun my fear into all the horrible things that might happen next. I don't know what shifted the moment in my favor. "I am an alpinist. I love your country and all the people I have met here. Please, help me get home to my family, to my mother, my father, my love." I believe my being a climber at least opened his mind to a less aggressive line of interrogation. This, combined with my consistent surrender to his authority, then my eventual shift to a position of asking for his help finally flipped the switch. His stare went distant. Blank was his face. I don't know where he was for the next few moments. I would call it an awkward silence, but it wasn't. It was a moment of detachment, floating through time, at a fork in my life when I knew I had no control in that moment. I was calm for the first time that day, in some deep way letting my fate go to him and beyond, while I waited for what was next. I didn't think about the fact that a real possibility could be the beginning of a long jail sentence, or perhaps being trapped for the rest of my life there, or execution, or a prison camp. It sounds quite dramatic looking back, but the truth is, crazier things happen every day in the shadows of the world. Especially in the lawless land of central Asia where you are constantly dancing between tranquility and terrorism, corruption and the next military coup, an amazing once-in-a-lifetime story and hell.

"Come with me." He broke the silence, not with a smile, but with a more relaxed posture. He didn't say whether I was going to be released or not, but I sensed in his energy and interaction with me that I was headed to freedom. Two-and-a-half hours of interrogation had passed. We made the long walk back down the hallway, then down the dark staircase, and back out into the afternoon air. A few minutes later, we were back to the primary building of the KGB in the small village where my driver Sultan and No Problem had been reunited. No Problem said, "Manfree, was problem, no problem Manfree. We free Manfree." Fortunately they had only scolded Sultan, letting him have it about dodging borders.

To this day, I'm still not sure how they knew we had circumnavigated some outpost and random border check points, but we were finally safely on our way as night fell.

Another incredible encounter with the rich culture of central Asia

That night we slept high in the mountains on the side of the road in the car, freezing.

The next morning, we arrived safely in Bishkek.

Vertical Momentum: From Insight to Action

"Once you finally get that summit, that's it then, right?"

I was shocked! This simple question from an audience member revealed a major gap in my content and message until that point. How had he missed that the summits never end? (Well, at least until we summit our last summit of life, which of course is our death, the ultimate summit.)

How we got down the Northwest Pillar of the Central Pyramid in the Aksu Valley, Kyrgyzstan is the obvious end of the story. What happened next in my life, and yours is not.

Summits are momentary, at best. We expend so much energy. So much stress. Stop. Start. Give up. Live up. And occasionally Step Up onto the summit. Then what?

We still have to get *down* safely, back to the valley below, and find our way home while never losing sight of the feeling of success, the power of possibility. This is often a critical turning point. Gravity, it seems, will be stronger than ever, pulling us toward complacency, no matter our previous triumphs. We must recover, reset, re-energize, regain momentum, and get ready for our next summit.

Recover: Be intentional. Schedule a long weekend and lower intensity work for a reasonable period of time, even if your life demands only allow a few days. We don't realize how much the pressure of achieving a new summit puts on our entire system. I've found that most often we dive right back into life-as-usual without building in any recovery time.

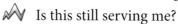 This is the part of the process that I see most often neglected, so beware and be ready to examine why *it's worth it for you* to take time to recover.

Reset: Stop before you start. The reset step is about wiping the slate as clean as possible before you dive back into anything. Reassess your commitments, specifically looking for items you can *stop before you start or restart.* Here are some questions to help you reset:

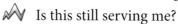 Is this still serving me?

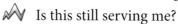 If I said no to this, what could it make room for?

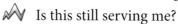 What in my life is most draining?

If you can't commit to stopping, give yourself permission to procrastinate a restart of the activity. Procrastination can be a powerful tool when used intentionally.

Re-energize: Embrace renewal activities *guilt-free*.

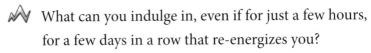 What can you indulge in, even if for just a few hours, for a few days in a row that re-energizes you?

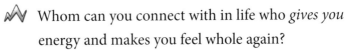 Whom can you connect with in life who *gives you* energy and makes you feel whole again?

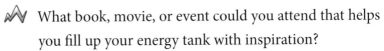 What book, movie, or event could you attend that helps you fill up your energy tank with inspiration?

Regain Momentum—Master the Art of the Restart Day-to-Day

This Vertical Lesson has proven to be the most profound mindset shift I've made in the last five years of my life. As with many of life's most insightful moments, the *aha* came at the intersection of wisdom from two of my key mentors. The mindset shift started with the teachings of my dear friend and business coach, Mark LeBlanc. Mark introduced the idea of tracking our activities towards our success in much smaller windows of time. As an example, instead putting all of our focus on a big annual goal, he encourages business owners to intensely focus on 30-day goals, with another sub-goal of daily activity to drive the results we are after. Mark teaches that we need to "reset our counters every thirty days and every twenty-four hours."

Me and Mark LeBlanc at his "Whatever It Takes" conference, La Jolla, California, September 27, 2015

Why is this way of thinking so powerful? I believe the magic comes from how quickly the opportunity to restart affects our daily lives, just as the opportunity to restart on our climb will present itself every time we fall or intentionally pause. This is exactly how I got through the morning of Day Three on the wall in Kyrgyzstan, as relayed in chapter 8.

The second part of the insight came August 22, 2015, with my speaking mentor and coach, Craig Valentine. I had flown up to Baltimore to spend an intensely focused four-hour session with Craig to get my new follow-up keynote to the next level. At one point early in the review of my keynote outline, I nonchalantly described a moment when my son fell on a climb, illustrated my point, then I moved on to the next scene in the story.

"What? Wait a second, did you say *he fell?*"

"Oh yeah, we fall a lot; we expect to fall." I responded.

"Did you say you *expect to fall? Really?*"

"Absolutely! That's how me make it up our most challenging climbs. You fall, hang there, recover, figure out the next few moves, and then climb on, restarting before you are completely ready."

The question is not *will we fall,* but *when we fall, what will we do next?*

I went on to explain to Craig how I'd been getting incredible results from Mark LeBlanc's parallel concept of resetting my life activity counters, and then the missing link hit me: our mindset in life is not the same as when we are climbing.

In life, I find that we put off the restart of key activities we know we need to build momentum until some major calendar event. Perhaps you've had the same experience. Let's take exercise as an example. This may come as a surprise, as most people see me and assume I just *love* to exercise, but the truth is I resist it as much as most people I know, and making it a consistent part of my life has been a constant struggle. I cannot count the number of times I've gotten all fired up about a new exercise activity, only to fall off the routine within a few months at best. I then tell myself, "well, I'll restart next month." Once I get near the end of the year, especially in the fourth quarter, I just blow off the restart until January 1. "I'll restart as a New Year's resolution; that'll work." Right.

We know how well those strategies work. But what if I did this when climbing? What if each time I fell, or had to hang on a piece of gear to recover, I put off restarting until the new month, or start of the new year? I'd never climb anything and I would die on the mountain, putting off the restart.

Me and Craig Valentine, 1999 Toastmaster World Champion and speech coaching guru

"Profound, Manley. Seriously, you need to explore this more. That is *not* how people typically think, and I can see how powerful this mindset could be. That's my big takeaway for the day: *Master the Art of the Restart.*" Craig's affirmation of the value of the insight encouraged me to further develop and share it with more audiences and clients in the months following, and it has quickly become a key lesson that's helping people build momentum every day.

When we climb, we expect to fall. We *Master the Art of the Restart* to ensure we build momentum on the climb, even if we are literally falling up the mountain. This is a very different mindset than what I had been operating with in my day-to-day life, and I believe it is the most powerful tool to build momentum I've ever implemented.

What if you approached your key daily activities with this mindset? Consider this: the next time you fall and blow your daily routine in any area of your life, accept the moment with a smile, greet your fall as an old friend you've been expecting to show up, and then commit to get on with it. "Of course, I fell! Tomorrow, I'll restart immediately." That's it. Immediately. Not at the beginning of the new month, quarter, or year, but *immediately.*

As soon as the sun comes up, *get on with it before you are ready.* This is another key insight to the *Art of the Restart*; when we are climbing, we can only see the next few moves in front of us. If we start thinking about all the challenges we'll face high above, we'd never have the courage to get moving again. Focus on the next few moves you need to start climbing again.

Here are the three essential steps to *Master the Art of the Restart* in your day-to-day efforts when you fall:

1. **Recall a previous summit:** Call back to *your last summit* in your next struggle

2. **Re-examine:** Figure out your *next* move

3. **Restart:** Get on with it *before* you are 100% ready

Regaining your momentum by *Mastering the Art of the Restart* in your day-to-day activities is especially useful as you come off a major climb in your life. Too often, everything goes by the wayside in the all-out effort to reach the summit, and we fall off our routine for many of our essential daily activities. Know that this mindset shift will reward you with momentum at any point in your journey ahead, and I recommend you work to embrace it every day, not just when you are in between major summits in your life.

SECTION THREE

Keep Climbing

CHAPTER 11

Vertical Lesson 9: Climb with Incredible Partners Only

It was my friend Travis who first planted the seed of climbing El Capitan in my mind, and his simple question about sleeping on walls altered my life experiences forever. Isn't it remarkable how just one person, planting the right seed when your mind is open and ready for growth, can dramatically change everything?

Looking back, I realize not just anyone telling me about El Capitan would have cast the magic spell on me that Travis did. It was his unrestrained passion that swept me up and onto the wall before he even finished the first sentence. To this day, I try to intentionally spend more time with people who are on fire with passion.

From 1992 to 1994, I fully immersed myself in climbing, obsessively filling every available moment with the pursuit of mastering it. If I had sixty minutes, I would go to the climbing gym in Lexington, Kentucky. If three hours or more were available, I'd make the one-hour drive to the Red River Gorge, even if it meant I only had an hour to get in one or two short climbs. I read every climbing book and magazine I could get my hands on over and over again. Every waking moment was filled with thoughts about climbing and the amazing places in the world where I could pursue The Vertical.

For college graduation, I asked my father for gas money to make a trip to California. My intent was to climb El Capitan. I joined forces with a regionally famous partner, Chris Snyder. Chris had lived in Yosemite and was fired up to get back out west. We made the journey to Yosemite, but never spent the night on El Capitan or any other big wall during that trip. For many years, I blamed Chris for not having the drive to get on El Capitan during our trip, but the truth is, he knew I was not ready and saved me the suffering.

Chris was smart to test my head as soon as we arrived. We climbed some moderate routes to warm up for the "big stone." I struggled to gain confidence and comfort on the foreign granite terrain, which was very different from the sandstone climbing I had learned on in Kentucky.

Chris Snyder on his route "8 Ball" deep in the steep sandstone of the Red River Gorge, Kentucky

Despite not getting on El Capitan that trip, it was a valuable journey. Chris introduced me to locals and gave me a crash course on the art of the "dirtbag lifestyle." I learned how climbers were able to amplify their quality of life with maximum time in The Vertical while maintaining a minimal standard of living. He taught me how to camp for free, where the cheap meals were, and showed me the hidden gems and sanctuaries of the park.

My experience with Chris prepped me for a nine-month odyssey the following year with my girlfriend, Emily. We lived out of the back of my small Toyota 2×4 truck, taking shelter under an aluminum topper, traveling throughout the Wild West on $300 a month. It was a tiny house on wheels and a reality show for real. That year, I learned that quality of life and standard of living are not directly correlated. We lived a simple life below the poverty line, and have yet to exceed the level of happiness we enjoyed that year, despite living more comfortably and materially enriched lives since. Early that spring, I made two trips to Yosemite and finally spent the night in The Vertical on my first big wall: a two-day effort to climb the Leaning Tower, in turbulent weather conditions with my climbing partner, Sean Easton.

The Leaning Tower is a 1200-foot overhanging granite wall in Yosemite National Park next to Bridalveil Falls that is considered the steepest big wall in North America.

Bridalveil Falls and the radically tilted Leaning Tower, Yosemite National Park, California

I stumbled upon Sean in a Yosemite parking lot. Little did I know his vision, skill, and willingness to suffer were a magic combination. We summited the Leaning Tower in dreadful weather, but had more fun that you would imagine hanging off the side of the earth cold, wet, and hungry.

My primary objective was to climb El Capitan that spring, but a relentless series of storms prevented Sean and two other partners I connected with from even touching the face of El Capitan. My quest continued.

It was two more years before I made my third pilgrimage across the country, in 1997. In my beater pickup truck, and this time dragging along an enthusiastic high school graduate, Grant Clouser, I set off for the hills of California. We arrived and quickly got on the Washington Column, a 1000-foot warm-up and right-of-passage for those who want to climb longer, more committing

The massively overhanging west face of the Leaning Tower. The West Face route follows a line directly up the center of the tower

Me drinking dessert on my first evening in The Vertical, on the Awanhee Ledge, a tiny space halfway up the steep west face of the Leaning Tower. Photo by Sean Easton, May 1995

walls like El Capitan. We spent two days on the wall, but Grant quickly succumbed to nerves and stomach issues. Looking back now, I realize how important getting in days and nights in The Vertical were; they had more impact on my momentum than you might expect. To summit is obviously most desirable, but don't underestimate the value of being on the wall climbing, even if you don't make it to the top. Consistent climbing out of your comfort zone and embracing the exposure of The Vertical, has a powerful cumulative effect.

Then I met partner number five, an enthusiastic, stocky young man I'll call "Smokey." Have you ever had a moment when you met a potential candidate for your team, and you really think you've found *the one*? I was convinced I had found my guy. Smokey was

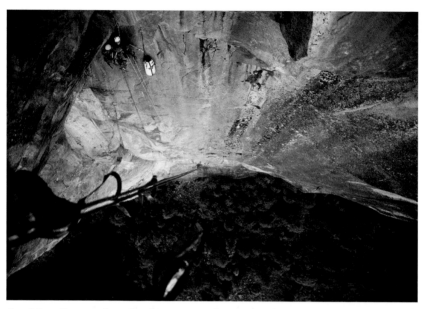

Looking down after climbing out a horizontal ceiling on the second day of my first big wall climb. You can see another climbing party, Sean Isaacs and friend, on their first big wall climb. May 1995

passionate and quite personable. His attitude was uplifting and optimistic, and after an evening with him, I was certain we would climb El Capitan together.

We planned to spend five days climbing and living on the wall. As with any project, figuring out what you need is a critical early step that can either facilitate success or bring your efforts to a grinding halt. In mountain climbing, a forgotten item can result in anything from an inconvenience to a life-threatening disaster. This exercise alone requires great care in strategy and execution. You must bring everything you need to live on the wall with you, dragging it up the stone and back down. What gear do you need to weather the conditions, and make safe and efficient progress to the summit and back before you run out of water and food? There are so

Coming up for air after enduring a late spring snow storm on my first portaledge bivouac on "Skull Queen," a two-day big-wall route on the Washington Column in Yosemite National Park, California. Photo by Jacob Sack, May 1995

many items to carefully consider. Shelter, climbing equipment, toilet paper, beer; the list of survival essentials is long, and the temptation to bring everything you might possibly need must be balanced with the reality that every additional pound will slow your progress.

Smokey and I spread our gear out on two tarps and started preparing. We had picked a route we thought was within our reach—"The Triple Direct." We consulted with local experts on strategy and the tactical climbing tools that would be needed and managed to gather all the equipment we believed would support our success. After two full days of planning and packing, we were ready for our first attempt on the great El Capitan.

The next morning, we hauled 200 pounds of gear to the base and stepped up into The Vertical on the southwest face of El Capitan. We employed standard aid climbing technique, following thin cracks in the granite that vary in size from the thickness of a kitchen knife, to the width of your head.

 Aid climbing: Using your safety gear to "aid" your upward progress, pulling on equipment you insert into the cracks in the rock because the rock is often too steep and difficult to advance merely using your hands and feet alone to grip the wall. Aid climbing gets the job done, but is a slow grind up the wall.

On the route we chose, we expected cracks typically averaging from a half-inch to three inches, and we had chosen our climbing

Grant Clouser, loaded down with half of our gear and ready for his first night in The Vertical on "The Prow," the Washington Column, Yosemite National Park, California, June 1997

gear accordingly. Since granite is typically smooth and featureless, the choice of gear to use in the crack systems is critical, proving to either be a showstopper or the perfect balance of the right tools to aid and protect your progress.

This was a milestone moment for me. The project had finally launched. I was actually climbing the object of my five-year dream. If anything, I would have expected the intimidation and fear I had felt all those years, dreaming from across the country and gazing up at El Capitan from the valley floor, to magnify. But the opposite happened. With each 150- to 200-foot section of climbing we successfully scaled, I felt significant momentum build. It seemed to be fueled by equal parts euphoria and confidence. For the first time ever, I realized I could actually climb this massive wall, one move at a time, one section at a time, one day at a time. This was a major mental turning point for me. However, as my momentum built, one major problem became obvious. It was Smokey.

By 1:30 p.m., we had ascended just more than five pitches of climbing, placing us 540 feet up the wall. I was elated. I should have known the three packs of cigarettes he had already burned down was a bad sign.

Smokey was freaking out. Shaking, sweating, and taking three cigarettes to get out three sentences, Smokey courageously called it out. "Manley…dude…man…uhh… <puff puff>…I, uh…<puff puff>…Manley, I'm not your guy. I ain't going to the top of this thing with you. I need to go down *now!*"

Disappointed? Actually, I was relieved! Thank goodness he called it out then, before we got truly committed. (How I wish moments like these in business were this easy.)

My experience with Smokey led me to an important interview question I used when I met partners six and seven. I remember

Smokey and me with our gear all sorted and ready to go the night before our launch onto El Capitan, June 1997

posing the killer question to Dave Lavallèe and Paul Midkiff two days later in the parking lot. "Are you willing to suffer?" They didn't even flinch.

I remember Dave looking me right in the eyes. "Of course! It's the only way we'll ever make it to the top! We're going to have a lot of fun too, but there will definitely be some suffering on our way to the summit. All worth it, Manley." I knew I had *Incredible Partners* this time, and after a five-day effort and multiple setbacks that would have sent most partners back to the comfort of the ground, we summited El Capitan together in June of 1997.

Vertical Momentum: From Insight to Action

Has it ever happened to you? You need someone *exceptional* for a position on your team. You meet them, and after an interview or two, you are convinced. Perhaps you even exuberantly share the news with your boss: "Oh, we've got a good one this time! This new hire is going to be the one that changes *everything*." Then a few months pass and the boss stops by for a "check-in."

"Hey, what is up with the new hire? I thought he was going to be amazing?"

To which you might reply, "Don't ask me, you thought he was great, too."

And then, does it go this way? Your Smokey walks in and calls it out. "Hey, boss, look, I've been thinking, I pretty much suck at this. You know, you really need to let me go. And until you get the paperwork all taken care of, cut my pay immediately."

Ha! Don't we wish it were that easy in business?

As you know, it rarely works that way. If you are like me, perhaps you've avoided some of those difficult conversations; hoping

Smokey, over five hundred feet up the southwest face of El Capitan, June 1997

Smokey would step up and improve. I know it's not easy, and I also know how damaging even one Smokey on your team can be.

What I have learned in the mountains and in business is, in order to bring about our very best results, we need to climb with *Incredible Partners Only*. Most anyone would agree with this statement.

Then where do we go wrong in executing this essential principle? With most organizations I work with, I find that their core values—what I call your *No Matter Whats*—have been compromised in one of three key areas.

$\wedge\!\!\!\wedge$ First, many are not crystal clear on exactly what their *No Matter Whats* are.

$\wedge\!\!\!\wedge$ Second, exceptions are often made during their partner selection process.

$\wedge\!\!\!\wedge$ Finally, and most frequently, the *No Matter Whats* are too often ignored in daily performance management.

Are the essential *No Matter What* core values of your organization visibly present in the activities and results of your team members every day? I encourage you to develop your own *No Matter What* list, keep it visible in the organization, and keep it alive and growing culturally by referring to it consistently in meetings and through day-to-day support, recognition, and praise of every individual.

When organizations have taken the time to work with me or others to gain clarity on not what they would *like* to have, but what they absolutely *must* have, it changes everything. Through my work, I have experienced hundreds of organizations with various cultural focus points, and each can be effective.

Dave Lavallèe committing in the face of sketchy weather on the southeast face of El Capitan on "The Zodiac," June 1997

In my decades of experience in The Vertical and business, I've spent countless hours trying to gain clarity on what essential values consistently produce exceptional results. I started noticing that the same values demonstrated by my *Incredible Partners* in The Vertical were the same values demonstrated by my *Incredible Partners* in business. Sometimes they were immediate team members, while others were in a completely different division, or external partners to the organization. Likewise, in my personal life, those who showed up as *Incredible Partners* for me were sometimes older and wiser, sometimes many years younger, sometimes family, or no relation, sometimes people I had known for years, and sometimes people who were relatively new to my life's journey.

What I did find in common were three core values that my *Incredible Partners* consistently pursued and demonstrated in their behaviors. I also observed that when any of these three core values were compromised, results always suffered measurably. I encourage you to consider these as a starting point, and then define your own *No Matter What* core values. If you will at least pursue these with an intentional and consistent focus in every action in your day to day leadership and management, they will provide you with a significant advantage.

1. **Passion.** Finding and cultivating passion is priority number one in my hiring process, along with day-to-day energy management in the workplace and personal life. Is the person *passionate* about *anything* in his or her life? Too often, I've had people sitting in front of me in an interview who have already passed initial HR screening and gone through competent interviewing processes and testing, but when I look for engagement and energy, they

Me ascending the steep south east face of El Capitan, with the thin crack of the Zodiac in the foreground, June 1997

are flat-lined. As Les Brown once said, "These people are already dead, they just haven't laid down yet." One of my favorite interview questions is simply, "What are you most passionate about?" I am not necessarily looking for a response related to the work they are being considered for, but any sign of fire in the belly. Something. As a leader, regardless of title, it is essential for you to stoke the fire, encourage and bring out the best in those around you. But give yourself something to work with!

Find the fire. No fire, no hire!

2. **People**. Are they people-service focused? Some people just don't like people. Do yourself a big favor and avoid them whenever possible. This can be especially difficult when the position requires someone exceptionally intelligent. It seems that many are intellectually brilliant, yet not people-service focused. For many teams, these partners can be critically important and necessary for the roles that must be filled. I'm not saying that everyone you hire must be a socializing extrovert. They can be introverted, intellectually brilliant, and still very effective. What I *am* saying is that it is essential that when you look people in the eyes and shake their hands, you know they *care*. When your team members and customers connect with them, do they get that they care? I believe we too often let jerks off the hook with, "Well, they just aren't a people person," or "They're just introverts." No jerks, no exceptions. I have worked with plenty of introverts who were delightful, caring people, and extroverts who were not service focused. A person's social orientation is no

Paul Midkiff and me waking up on our portledge at the top of "The Zodiac," with only sixty feet of the final pitch to the summit of El Capitan. Photo by Kennan Harvey.

excuse for not living up to the people-service focused value. If they aren't able to connect and show care for people, let someone else have them.

I see this constantly, and I have made the same mistake myself. A person has the technical skill set and experience needed, but I don't feel like their people skills are where they need to be. So, I bring them onto the team, convinced I can "fix" or "train" the people skills. What I have found is these skills certainly can be constantly developed, but as with the *Passion* factor, you have to give yourself something to work with! Even if they are not customer-facing, you and your internal teams are going to have to deal with them every day. Internal friction can create significant disruptions to productivity and poison your culture. Ultimately, all team member interactions affect your customers and your bottom line.

Do they care? When you, your team and your customers know and feel it, they all show up differently. Workplace collaboration increases, customers are more likely to come back, and everyone goes home with less stress at the end of the day.

3. **Perseverance.** So what was missing with Smokey? Passion? No; he was passionate, enthusiastic, and energized with the attitude it takes to accomplish something that's beyond your comfort zone. People-service focused? Oh, yeah, he had this too. Smokey was a kind, fun, friendly and service-focused person. So what was missing? Perseverance. When the going got tough Smokey folded.

Me on lead pulling the last move of our five day big wall climb, with Dave on belay below. Photo by Paul Midkiff.

Are you willing to suffer? How do you respond in the face of adversity, overwhelming odds and challenge? Most people are not ready to step up and contribute in a culture of high performance. Having interview questions, assessments, and conversations with references that focus on uncovering this critical factor can be a game-changer. I know what you are thinking. "Really? I should ask someone if they are 'willing to suffer'?" No; probably not HR-approved, but what question could you ask to get a sense of a candidate's willingness to operate in uncomfortable scenarios? How can you get a sense of their *resilience*? Passion? People-service focus?

Clearly Define Your *No Matter Whats*

What are your *No Matter What* core values?

In the early years of my business life, I went about leading, hiring, developing, and overcoming challenges with my teams without great clarity regarding the essential values required to get the results. Understanding what values were essential and would lead to incredible results came through trial and error, struggles, and success in the trenches.

Now, you have the advantage of taking a step back, gaining clarity, and pursuing these values in the teams you build going forward. I invite you to first invest in the time to clearly establish your *No Matter Whats*. You do not have to be the manager or supervisor of a team to benefit from clarifying and committing to your *No Matter Whats*. On a personal level, they form the foundation of the microculture you create in your personal sphere of influence, ensuring that you are showing up, speaking up, and

Dave, Paul, and me on the summit of El Capitan, June 1997

stepping up as an *Incredible Partner* every day. Next, repeat the process with your team and important people in your life.

Here is a step-by-step process to gain clarity on your *No Matter Whats*:

1. Brainstorm one- or two-word phrases that capture core values that are critically important to you.

   Examples: Passion, integrity, hardworking, accountable, service-focused, resilient

   You don't need a long list for this to be effective. Less is more. Only keep words that you feel *deeply* committed to living up to with your actions, *no matter what.*

2. Group similar words, then pick the one that resonates most with you. The synonyms can be used in the next step

when describing what the word means to you and how the word shows up in the behaviors you'll strive to commit to every day.

3. Draft a few sentences about each word that capture:

    ⋀⋀ Why is the word is important to you?

    ⋀⋀ What does the word look like in action when demonstrated in your behaviors?

    ⋀⋀ Why is it *worth it* to pursue the value?

4. Review and refer to the document when making decisions and taking important actions, such as hiring, performance reviews, day-to-day meetings, prioritizing focus, resolving ethical dilemmas, etc.

5. Review and update your *No Matter Whats* at least once a year.

Never Compromise Your *No Matter Whats*

Are you honoring your *No Matter Whats* in your partner selection process?

We were getting desperate. Like many organizations, our Build-A-Bear IT team was struggling to fill an important technical position. Finally, we found a candidate. I'll call him Big Jer. On the technical side, he was exceptionally competent and made it through all of our IT manager interviews despite his lack of people skills. Then he sat down with our CFO, Mrs. Tina Klocke. Miss Tina, as I affectionately called her, had a favorite interview question. "What do you think of our stores?"

Big Jer's response was, "I've never been to one of your stores." More shocking was his response to her next question.

"Are you going to visit a store?" Tina responded.

"If you give me an offer, I'll consider it."

Wow!

Needless to say, Miss Tina refused to sign off on hiring Big Jer. We even pushed back, citing his intellectual brilliance, extensive technical skill set, and our urgent need to finally fill the position. We challenged her, saying, "he won't be working with our customers, Tina; it's ok that he's not up to our people-service-focused-value standard." I'll never forget her response.

"Do you want to work with him? I know I don't."

She was absolutely right, and saved us from compromising our *No Matter Whats*. Whether you are selecting a team member, a vendor, or a partner for The Vertical, having other people you trust and who understand your *No Matter Whats* evaluate the person you are considering can help ensure you select *Incredible Partners Only*. Be sure to review your *No Matter Whats* throughout the selection process, including having the potential partner review them.

Commit to Pursuing Your *No Matter Whats* Every Day

My final question is, are your *No Matter Whats* currently on fire in you and those surrounding you?

It just takes one Smokey to hold you, your entire team, if not your entire organization back. I encourage you to do two things. First, step back on a regular basis and honestly ask, "Who is my Smokey?" Typically, at any given time, there will be at least one team member, or person in your life who is not bringing his or her best. Am I saying you need to fire this person? Not necessarily. One thing is clear, ignoring the situation only makes matters worse. The second step is the hardest. Have the courage to call it out, and *challenge the individual to step up or step out.*

If you put off those critical conversations, as I have done, it never gets easier. It always drags your team down. Just one Smokey exponentially increases the drag of gravity on all your efforts. I know when you are out there and looking for people, you're probably saying, "Man, you don't know what I have to choose from. You know what, Manley? If they are breathing and sober, we're going to have to give them a shot." I know some job markets are very challenging, but don't give in. Resist the temptation to compromise your *No Matter Whats*. When you start with core values of *passion, people* and *perseverance*, and select team members with those three values strongly represented, you will build on a foundation than can support an exceptional high performance culture; a culture that will produce more engagement, more accountability, more collaboration, and more innovation. You will find yourself and your teams showing up, speaking up, and stepping up to realize more of what is possible.

CHAPTER 12

Leaving Your Legacy

Now what?

You've come this far in your life, and you've endured this expedition with me, gaining many insights to help you on your life expedition in the days and years ahead. There's one major obstacle that now stands in the way of you truly realizing your next summit. I know this obstacle well, as I've watched it rob me of potential in my life too many times to mention.

You've had a moment of clarity. Your awareness sharpened by exposure to ideas that have inspired you to step up. You know what to do next—how shifts in your mindset and tweaks to your tactics will yield momentum and more of what you seek in your efforts.

But then it happens.

Have you ever experienced the moment I just described? Maybe it was a meaningful book in your hands, or perhaps you saw a speaker, or a sermon, or a movie that engaged your mind, filled your heart with hope, and stirred you spirit to soar. You were ready. Fired up. Determined that life was going to be better than before. Then, three weeks or even three months later, you have the realization that you are stuck in the same place you'd been before that moment of clarity and empowerment. Frustrating, and unavoidable if we don't examine and then deepen your commitment and understanding of why changing is *worth it* to you.

This is the crux of it all. We have no shortage of great information. Just Google anything you want to know right now; almost anything you want is there. Why, then, despite having access to the *how*, do we not shift our mindsets and behavior into new patterns that serve us more effectively? Because we are humans, and changing human behavior is not easy.

I've found that the key is to get in touch with *why* it would be *worth it* for us to move forward. Aren't you busy already? Feel overwhelmed with things to do, places to be, people to serve? And now I've asked you to do something differently—to leverage new strategies and tools to reach your next summit. Is it really *worth it*?

I was examining this key question in the spring of 2014, through the lens of leadership. Until then, the word "leadership" had occupied a very traditional existence in my belief system: someone, typically with some authority, getting others to do what they want or need them to do. Think boss and employee or commander and troop or appointed position and volunteer. And then an unexpected event in my life completely shifted my perspective and challenged my previously held beliefs and definitions.

Above all else, this is the part of the story I wish everyone on your team and in your life could hear right now. In 2008, I made another journey to a majestic cathedral of creation, Yosemite Valley, California. I travelled across the country with my dear friend, Josh Hawkins, with a goal in mind. Our intention was to climb El Capitan in Yosemite, following the original route up the wall, the historic "Nose." Applying what I had learned in 1997 on my first El Capitan climb, I decided to apply my *Incredible Partners Only* principal. I lined up a third incredible partner to form a team of three, increasing our odds of success.

I knew exactly what we needed in the third team member. Someone with significant experience living on the massive walls of El Capitan. A partner who was passionate, people-focused, and someone who would persevere when the inevitable challenges came. After several months of connecting with friends in the climbing community, I lined up an old climbing friend, Rich Copeland, to be our third partner.

Before we knew it, the two years of planning had passed and we were driving through the long Wawona tunnel into Yosemite Valley, finally awestruck with infamous Discovery View, a panorama of earth in its finest glory. Waterfalls, blue sky, massive granite walls, green meadows. The elegant Half Dome sits in the distance watching over the valley. On your left, the enormous and largest wall guards the valley and her people. We made our way down to the meadows across from El Capitan, a delightful field of grass surrounded by serene beauty. This is the place where many people come to gaze and dream, or plan and pack for their adventure. Most are there to simply walk on foot on the extensive network of day trails, able to enjoy the stunning beauty of the park with minimal physical fitness and commitment, only to relax and take it all in. On the other end of the adventure spectrum, you have people from around the world who have come to chase down their dream: climbing what is considered to be one of the most demanding and significant rock-climbing test pieces on the planet, El Capitan.

Rich celebrating our arrival at Yosemite, 2008

Josh and I came with a goal, but Rich showed up with a vision. Leaders don't need a title to do this, and Rich certainly had no title with us, but his ability to express a vision bigger than our goal was in full motion before the end of our first day. Rich said, "I know you all want to climb the Nose, but there's a new route that's only been climbed one time. It has some serious and difficult new climbing, much harder than the Nose route. It's called *Atlantis*. It would be an incredible experience."

It didn't take me long to think about his crazy idea. I quickly responded, "You are crazy, Rich! No way!"

Then Rich did something great leaders do. He saw potential in us—something we did not see or believe in ourselves. Then he illuminated our strengths—at first to simply ignite our imagination. Then, slowly but surely, Rich breathed more life into our imagination until it grew into a belief that we held as possible. I remember the conversations vividly. "I know your climbing ability, Manley. You can do this. And you too, Josh. I don't care how long you've been climbing; we got this." Josh was relatively new to the sport at this time, but his full-on assault and fearless approach to everything I threw at him in his first year on the rock was stunning. Josh was wisely apprehensive, and Rich's nonchalant approach to life didn't help his confidence.

We then met up with Rich's dear friend and extraordinarily accomplished big-wall master, Erik Sloan. At the time of this printing, Erik has more than 100 El Capitan summits under his belt, and he's the coauthor of the comprehensive guidebook to the wall. If anyone could give us objective guidance on what route would be best for us to take, it would be Erik.

He made his opinion clear in the first five minutes, and an alternative plan emerged. Erik and Rich proposed the idea of splitting into two teams. "Rich and Manley should bag the second ascent of Atlantis, and Josh and I will have more fun on the Nose while you all suffer. We can all meet on top and celebrate together."

I was concerned with the idea of us dividing and conquering. I knew it was a grand plan, and all would be content *if* both teams made the summit.

Our new plans were set into motion. The next day we were lucky enough to meet up with Dave Turner, an extraordinary young talent in the climbing world. In September of 2005, Dave had completed the first and only ascent of Atlantis up one of the steepest and blankest walls on the entire face of El Capitan. Together we sat for hours in the Yosemite cafeteria while Dave hand-drew a map of the route from memory on piece of scrap paper, talking us through the complex logistics of planning our vertical expedition.

After planning on paper, it was time to sort and pack our gear in the traditional spot. We spread our tarp in El Capitan Meadows, sorting through a mess of possible options to narrow our list to our best calculation and guess about what it would take for safe passage. (In Yosemite, this process is called *the junk show*. The phrase stuck after fellow-climbers would wander by and say, "Nice junk show! What are you all getting ready for?" Often, someone who may have climbed your intended route will offer their thoughts on everything from your choice of beer to the brand of toilet paper, or even relevant advice on gear selection. The junk show process is a delicate balance between having everything you might need and over-packing. You must choose every ounce with great caution. What if you forego a critical tool you need? What if you come up short on supplies? You could have an instant epic and even find

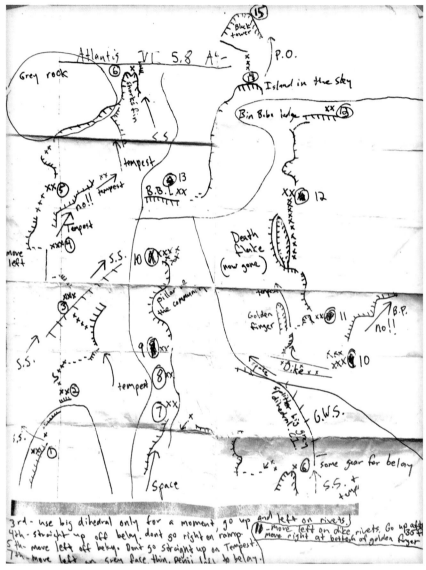

Dave Turner's hand-drawn map of Atlantis that we used for our
second ascent attempt

Rich and Dave doing the junk show, meticulously selecting everything we needed to survive on the side of El Capitan for fourteen days

yourself struggling for your life. On the other hand, if you pack too much, your progress may be so slow that you never reach your summit.)

After a full day sorting through the junk show, we had all of our supplies, including our best estimate of all the food, water and essentials it would take to survive on the wall for fourteen days. This was a dramatic shift from our original plan to climb The Nose route in three to five days. Not only were more days of supplies needed, but the equipment that the cutting-edge route demanded also significantly added to our overall weight. After shuttling multiple loads of gear to the base of the route, we had our 500 pound junk show packed and ready. The next day, we launched into The Vertical.

Rich launching into The Vertical of Atlantis, on the massive and steep south west face of El Capitan, September 23, 2008

Rich handling a lead on day two with Middle and Lower Cathedral Walls below

In contrast to my climbing in Kyrgyzstan, our ascent of Atlantis was so technically difficult that we would be using *aid climbing* style to ascend. We built good momentum the first two days of the climb, taking turns leading the rope past long sections of granite with micro-features in the rock we could barely hang on to. Imagine small cracks you might see in a sidewalk or foundation of a house. Our all-out, anything-goes climbing style depended on using a massive arsenal of tools to ascend the extremely challenging wall, hanging on edges thinner than a pencil and following cracks just wide enough to fit a knife blade in. Three things became clear very quickly on the route. The physical demands of the route were pushing our body to the limit every day. The mental load of the intensely difficult climbing was stretching us well outside of our comfort zone. And thirdly, we were having more fun than you can imagine, fueling our slow

Rich on lead, with a good view of the steep exposure of El Capitan sweeping behind him

grind up the wall with humor and self-generated happiness. Every day, we knew we had an incredible amount of work in front of us, and more uncertainty than I can typically stomach. We knew that we got to do one thing we truly love; live on the edge of the planet in The Vertical, focused on one sole objective. Up, up, always up, live to tell, and make it back down alive.

The climbing was by far the most difficult I had ever endured, and on the outer edge of Rich's comfort zone as well. Then a serious test came my way on Day Three. It was my turn to lead up the left side of an infamous feature on the wall, the shark's tooth. Six hours on lead and then two feet from the anchor, my foot became stuck in a crack. It was midnight and I was beyond exhausted. Even my emergency adrenaline reserve tank seemed to be tapped out. I wanted to finish that last move so badly, but Rich encouraged a more sensible alternative to me beating my body against the wall. He talked me into creating an anchor at my high point, "fixing the line" and descending back down to our hanging camp. This would prove to be a decision that nearly cost Rich his life.

The morning of Day Four came sunny and beautiful, but we were beat. Rich rallied large and headed up on the line I had established late the night before. Half the way up, I heard Rich's entire demeanor change, and I got a rare glimpse into Rich's world when he was full of fear. "Oh my God. Oh my God! Holy shit! Oh wow!"

"*What!* What is it?" I yelled up to him.

"Dude, the rope blew in behind a flake overnight, and it is nearly worn through." The previous night's wind had, in fact, blown the rope into a space in the granite where it had gotten stuck; unbeknownst to us, as Rich had started climbing, the rope was grinding against a sharp, knifelike edge with every step. By the time

Rich Copeland recovering from a day in The Vertical on "Atlantis," El Capitan, September 2008

he got there it was nearly cut in half. "The sheath of the rope is gone and it looks like the core of the rope is failing," he called out. Rich was one hundred feet up and out to my right, spinning in space, with no way for me to help him. We talked through very limited options while we got sick to our stomachs. "I'm just going to have to get past it, take my time and ascend as deliberately as possible to minimize the wear."

This was perhaps the longest twenty minutes of my life, watching, waiting, and praying for Rich's safe passage past the compromised point of the rope. With grace, before we knew it, the surreal moment had passed and Rich was again safe. By the time Rich safely passed the cut part of the rope, more than 1/2 of the core fibers had cut through. We each stuffed a piece into our pockets to keep as a reminder and chopped off the wound. This shortened our haul line by about 65 feet, but still left us with enough to finish the route.

This moment was probably a good mental warm-up, as Rich was up for the next pitch—the crux of the entire wall. Dave had spent nearly an hour talking about this especially blank stretch of wall, walking Rich though a delicate strategy that would enable him to traverse over, up, and then back down nearly 200 feet. The most unnerving part of the pitch was the fact that if the leader fell, he would likely come swinging like a pendulum back into the shark's fin, a massive slab of granite pasted onto the side of El Capitan. The shark's fin had allowed our passage by carefully climbing the crack between it and the wall, but now it created a dangerous protruding hazard for Rich. After four-and-a-half hours, Rich finally finished the extraordinary section of climbing.

Rich ascending the damaged fixed rope on the morning of Day Four,
Atlantis

(You can see video footage and incredible photos of this pitch on ReachingYourNextSummit.com. Hearing Rich after he finishes climbing the crux alone, is worth the trip to the page right now. It will put a smile on your face.)

Finishing Day Four gave us hope and momentum. We felt a distinct positive shift after Rich survived a close call ascending our fixed line, and then his delicate dance through the difficulties of pitch seven positioned us with the technical crux of the route behind us. We knew our next morning would lead us through the last of the new route territory, where we would merge onto an older route, "Space." Rich took the morning lead, making good progress through beautiful and clean granite above us. After climbing through the end of the new vertical territory Atlantis charted, Rich began a traverse on micro edges. The climbing was tricky and tested his patience, but eventually he found a hidden edge and made the second-to-last dicey move.

PING! The loud noise of metal shearing off the granite blended quickly with Rich's grunt as he starting falling. I immediately locked off his rope and braced for the impact of his body coming back to the Captain. His impact with the wall was sickening. The sunny, peaceful warm morning was torn open as Rich's foot caught a small feature on the wall. He moaned in agony and slowly beat his helmet and head against the wall, twisting in excruciating pain on the end of the rope. His body came to rest 100 feet above me, and I immediately yelled up for some hope that he was OK, knowing he wasn't. "You OK, brother?"

"My ankle is destroyed, Manley. I'm in so much pain!"

I immediately lowered Rich back down to our portaledge. Grimacing in pain, Rich first slowed his breathing so he could speak. "Manley, you remember those beers we saved for the summit?"

Rich heading out on the crux pitch of Atlantis, Day Four

I said, "Yes sir!"

With an enthusiastic and twisted smile, he said, "I need one now!" I jumped into action, diving deep in our haul bag, and within minutes had a warm beer in his hands. It gave a moment of minor relief; enough time for us to start the difficult process of figuring out what we were going to do next. We had two options. The first one was really obvious and most sensible. In Yosemite, they have the most advanced vertical rescue team in the world. With a simple cell phone call, a ground team immediately is set into action, while an air team is dispatched from military bases on the West Coast. Within a few hours, a helicopter-based team, typically support from both the ground and summit operations, plucks you off the wall. Before you know it, you can be at the mountain bar sipping on a cold beer.

"Well, we could call for a rescue, but I like option two better, Manley." I just started staring at Rich, trying to be supportive and ready for anything he asked.

"What's option two?"

"Manley, option two is we get ourselves down. A self-rescue. It would be much better style."

"Style? Rich, you are crazy!"

As he had done on the ground, again Rich secretly broke out his leadership influence tools and inspired me, starting first with a sincere expression of his belief in me. "Manley, I know we can do it. Now, I know I'm not gonna be a lot of help."

I said, "Yeah, I know. No offense, but that's what I'm worried about! I can't get us off this wall with you incapacitated!"

"I promise I won't complain. We will get down with you leading us. You totally have the skills to get us down from here,

Rich halfway through the crux pitch of Atlantis, with me on belay.
Photo by Tom Evans.

Rich digging deep and ready to finish his lead of the crux pitch of Atlantis.

Manley. We don't need a rescue." I objected, pointing out that Rich's ankle was most certainly broken, based on the noise he heard on impact and how swollen it was already—a softball-sized bulge had blown out around the joint.

"Seriously brother, you got this. I have complete faith that you can get us down. We'll have Erik and Tom and our friends on the ground help us navigate. They'll have a better perspective and help us avoid rappelling off the end of our ropes."

It's a fact that big-wall climbing is a ton of work—the most purely labor-intensive and least glamorous of all climbing styles. Moving up or down on a big wall with a competent team takes extraordinary effort and skill. With only one person doing the work, the actual labor increase is four times the work of having a

Rich roped up and on lead on the morning of Day Five

two-person team. But my resistance wasn't about the extra work, and Rich knew it, addressing my biggest fear head on. We both knew what our biggest risk was, and it was the exact fear that was fueling my resistance.

We were most fearful of navigating down the incredibly steep wall through new, unknown terrain. Finding anchors left behind by previous climbing parties is just a bit easier than looking for a needle in a haystack. In the visual realm of thousands of square feet of granite, you are looking for gray, steel-colored bolts with a loop that you clip the team into. On granite, they are very well camouflaged. Of course, as any great leader would be, Rich was fully aware of our fears, both real and imagined, and Rich systematically took the time to explore all of them through as much conversation as needed. Additionally, just as he had on the ground, he had a vision of what was possible. For the remainder of the day, he leveraged the trust of our relationship. Rich inspired and influenced me, finally convincing me to attempt a self-rescue. I knew it was going to be an epic effort. Getting Rich and all of our gear to the ground, using only our own limited power with no direct assistance was way beyond my comfort zone.

The next morning, Day Six on the wall, we struggled to descend the massively overhanging wall with Rich's broken ankle and escape with all of our gear. One of the biggest challenges was the logistical navigation, as our retreat required we take a new, more direct line down the wall than our ascent to that point had followed. The only reason this became safe instead of terrifying was the help we had from the ground. Led by our friend Erik, who knows El Capitan as well as anyone in the world, and aided by Tom Evans' knowledge and photography gear, we were able to have them

Rich seconds before his 35-foot lead fall, which left him hanging at the lower arch in the photo. Photo by Tom Evans

Rich back on the portaledge, contemplating pain and style after his fall, our fifth evening in The Vertical

help guide our way, ensuring we hit micro-targets on the wall, using anchors to relay our equipment and Rich down safely.

Perspective played a big part in our success. Most often, when you are on the climb, in the struggle, your perspective is dramatically skewed. By trusting our ground support team to lead our blind descent back to earth, we were able to have no major mishaps. It took a tremendous physical effort, all the courage Rich and the ground team could give me, and absolute trust in their guidance. *I trusted them because I knew they were competent, and that they cared for us. I listened to them because I knew they had perspective that we did not.*

As the last light fell below the horizon, we connected with our final major anchor. This was the exact point our full commitment

Rich bringing joy to a desperate situation, airing out his ankle and smiling for Tom's camera in the meadow below. Photo by Tom Evans.

to the wall nearly a week before had started. It took two hours of navigating the final void in the dark, and then we were at the base safely, finally able to stand on earth again after six long days in The Vertical. We regrouped and then Rich crawled on his hands and knees back to the car. This took more than two hours; a journey typically made in twenty minutes.

Our experience on the wall has continued to inform my life in many surprising ways. You would think the focus of the reflection might be the actual climb, its difficulty, our self-rescue, or the sheer insanity of living on an ocean of granite for nearly a week. But that's not what stuck with me most about those days. What has affected me most is Rich. And I'm not talking about how competent he was (he most certainly was). His skill at finding a safe passage up impossible looking stretches of granite was exceptional. His superhuman strength, willpower, and ability to deal with pain was outrageous. All of which are worthy characteristics. What sticks with me most about the experience is how Rich connected with me in such a humble and human way. He showed up to serve first in his actions. When there were two big loads to carry, he just grabbed the heavier one. When there were two portions of food, he always just grabbed the smaller one. When just a little water remained in a bottle, he made sure I got all of it, even when we were both thirsty. What is even more remarkable is that it wasn't just me. I witnessed how he engaged every person on the ground, day after day. He seemed to impact every individual he encountered in a positive way, lifting and lighting them up when they saw him.

Do you know anyone like that? One of those people with whom, when your paths cross, you connect in a meaningful way?

Looking down at our last portaledge camp before starting our self-rescue

And then you walk away, feeling enlightened and energized. You are simply better than you were before that moment. Rich is one of those people. Reflecting back on living with him on the wall day in and day out, in the quiet moments between the chaos, I realized Rich is a leader. At first I resisted this thought, as Rich did not fit my previous definition of a leader.

It was May 20, 2014. I had just finished a workshop at a National Intelligence and Defense Agency, forced to leave my cell phone in the car all day. Of course, the first thing I did after some valuable unplugged time was frantically reconnect to the world. My phone came up, and a text message from my dear friend and climbing partner Josh Hawkins was on top. It read, "Hey, did you hear about Rich?"

I was ready to drive home and felt an urgent sense to know what this meant. I focused on the realistic possibility that Rich had pulled off another incredible climbing feat, and I couldn't wait to hear. But the truth is, my immediate gut response was not good. Swimming against an undercurrent of anxiety, I called Josh immediately as I got on the highway in downtown St. Louis. "Josh, what's going on?"

There was a long silence, deepening my concern. "You didn't hear?"

"No, what? What's up with Rich? Tell me he climbed something amazing Josh!"

"No. Rich was up on a ledge getting ready for a climb in Yosemite on Sunday, and somehow—we don't know what happened, but he slipped off a ledge and he's gone."

"What! How?"

"No one knows. He wasn't even climbing. And it was a

A view from El Cap Meadow as we begin our self-rescue effort. Photo by Tom Evans.

Me and Rich Copeland in the woods below El Capitan, September 2013. Photo by Chris West.

massive ledge at the base of a wall. It appears to be a freak accident."

I was stunned. I felt an immediate swell of dread and grief sweep through me. I pulled off the next exit I encountered, and then just drove. Strangely enough, randomly following city streets led me to a dead-end street at a Catholic church downtown. I was raised Catholic, and had found comfort in the church during trying times as a child. I took this as something more than a random event and parked my car. The church was locked, so I just sat outside in the sun and reflected on Rich and how much my relatively brief moments with him had meant.

What happened next was stunning and inspired me deeply, further clarifying a new definition of what it means to lead in our lives every day. In 2014, I attended two funerals. One was a prominent businessman at a Fortune 50 company with which you most certainly are familiar. This man had a great leadership title. He died with a lot of money, a beautiful home, and all the details that surely would further align with what I thought of as a successful leader. I remember sitting in the church during the service and my wife, Emily, leaning over quietly to whisper in my ear. "Strange. The church is empty."

A few weeks after Rich's fall in Yosemite, I attended his funeral in Bridgeton, Missouri, a humble blue-collar neighborhood in St. Louis County. The funeral home was packed, standing room only. Friends from his childhood, high school, and his time as a factory worker at Ford gathered to share stories of how his life had impacted them. They talked about how Rich showed up every day of his life, and his incredible energy. His friends and family shared the attitude of joy with which Rich had met being laid off from his blue-collar career. Rich's layoff triggered him to act on the fire that had been growing in his heart for years, and led him to move to the Sierra mountains in California. He dedicated the rest of his life to introducing people to the wilderness. He traded comfortable city living for a basic small camping trailer in the mountains and went to work at Montecito Sequoia Lodge, a year-round retreat designed to enable families to reconnect to each other through an intimate and wild experience within an extraordinary area of the planet.

In Rich's years at the lodge, his impact grew immeasurably. This was evident on the internet in the wake of his death. Tribute pages went up on multiple climbing forums and Facebook. People from around the world posted photos of their meaningful moments with Rich. One showed a young teenager and Rich on a trail. The young man is a grown man now, and he wrote how Rich has profoundly impacted his life by introducing him to the outdoors. He is one of many who will forever be inspired by Rich.

After Rich's funeral in St. Louis, his many friends at the Montecito Lodge had a ceremony to honor him. A few days later, there was a third celebration of Rich's life in Yosemite Valley, in the meadow below El Capitan. People just kept showing up, everywhere, it seemed, to celebrate Rich's legacy. In addition to the multiple gatherings in his honor across the country; those touched by Rich refused to let his impact fade away. At the Montecito Lodge, every new group of people who came in, week after week, were enriched with stories of their fallen hero. And every week, they posted a group photo, adding a small stone in memory of Rich to the memorial they created at the lodge.

Wow. That is impact. That is legacy. And I believe that is leadership.

Sometimes we don't know one's influence and impact until we are left without it.

That's when it really hit me.

Here's what I wish everyone on your team, in your organization, connected to your life, could truly embrace right now.

Leadership is not about your title. It's not about how many people report to you or how much money you have. I believe the truest measure of a leader is the legacy he or she leaves.

Here's my final question for you. *What legacy will you leave?*

How would your life change if you contemplated that question for a few minutes every month?

What legacy will you leave?

I think that's what it's about.

If we are still here, there is still something left for us to give. When we see what is possible, we can't settle for the way things are. Then we commit—to show up, speak up and step up, into The Vertical of our lives, and reach for our next summit.

I cannot wait to hear about *your next summit*!

On Belay for life,

Manley

ABOUT THE AUTHOR

Manley is recognized as an award-winning international keynote speaker and business leader, author, published outdoor adventure photographer, and professional musician. He served two terms as the President of the National Speakers Association, St. Louis chapter.

During Manley's eleven years with Build-A-Bear Workshop, his leadership direction helped take the revolutionary retail concept from forty stores to over 400 worldwide, realizing revenue growth from 55 million to over 474 million, and a successful IPO on the NYSE. He built an award-winning reputation for implementing business solutions and support that produced measurable results every day. Manley's leadership influence contributed to a workplace culture that landed Build-A-Bear on the Fortune 100 Best Companies to Work For® List four years in a row.

It is this expertise that he shares by applying lessons learned in business and adventures to life's daily challenges. The authentic, sincere, and deep interpersonal connection Manley makes with an audience enables him to deliver practical and proven content to help organizations maximize their opportunities and develop their most valuable assets—their employees. Through custom-developed programs and support ranging from sixty minutes to a full year, he will leave you with many actionable techniques, frameworks, and insights. Most importantly, he can engage your organization in a way that sustains true results that last well beyond the presentation, and ultimately affect long term change.

Manley's inspirational keynotes are brought to life through his national geographic photography and riveting stories culminating from a lifetime of adventure through 25 countries, to over 400 outdoor destinations. Manley vividly shares compelling lessons from his adventure and leadership experiences in a way that allows you to relate to your mountains. He will have you hanging beside him surviving in the Himalayas, struggling to communicate in Uzbekistan, and immediately transferring the experience to moving you forward in your courageous efforts. Manley will challenge your mindset, arm you with ideas you can use, and inspire you to action.

On a personal note, Manley likes to sleep on the side of mountains. Even more shocking is that his wife has been putting up with that since 1993, and he has two teens that still kiss him on the cheek in front of their friends.

Manley relaxing on the edge of The Vertical near St. Louis, MO. 2015. Photo by Keith Lee Studios.

ACKNOWLEDGEMENTS

At great risk of missing someone important, I narrow the scope of these acknowledgements to those who've helped me along my path into The Vertical and onto these pages.

I am grateful for my late dear mother, Patricia Ann Deatherage. My mother taught me to dream bigger, believe more, and to have faith in love and God. She convinced me that I could do anything I wanted and lit the fire that keeps me going today.

I am grateful for my father, Manley version 1.0. My father has taught me to be kind and love everyone you encounter, to always pursue integrity, and that optimism trumps all. Your support helped make my adventures possible, including my experience in Kyrgyzstan and so many beautiful days at sea with you, Dianne, and our family that we will never forget. Thank you, Dianne, for being a mother to me and Emily, a grandmother to my children, and my father's soulmate.

I am grateful for my late dear mother-in-law, Sarah Roush. Sarah challenged me to step fully into my passion and always pursue my heart song. I am grateful for my father-in-law, Jim Roush, my base camp doctor and chef, who made sure I had the food and medicine I needed to make it back home alive.

I am grateful for Mark Williams, who introduced me to the wilderness and The Vertical, changing my life forever. To my early partners in the Red River Gorge, Travis Moore, Keith Moll,

Chris Snyder, Jeff Moll, Jeff Ashley. To my dear lifelong friends, Jeff Dickerson and Blaine Hamilton, who followed me anywhere I dared in my early adventures into The Vertical. I am grateful for Jeff Curry, Greg Dunn, and my other Vertical partners during my time in Paducah.

I am grateful for all my climbing partners on the big walls and mountains of the world: Sean Easton, Jacob Sack, Mark Deglomine, Jim Walters, Grant Clouser, Smokey, Paul Midkiff, Dave Lavallée, Matt, Josh Denys, Dima and Jula, Jody Burton, Ben Heath, Jersey Dave Litman, Josh Hawkins, and Rich Copeland.

I am grateful to my dear late friend Craig Sims. You pushed me to be a better man when no one is looking. You taught me that every moment of every day, from work to the woods, can be a blast. I am grateful for my days at Hooper's Outdoor Center, where Craig and Vicki Sims, Dean Cherry, Dave Hinkle and Mike Glover gave me a hands-on business education that has continued to help me serve others while pursuing adventure in every opportunity.

I am grateful for my dear friend and partner in The Vertical, Josh Hawkins. You continue to inspire me in so many ways. I constantly look forward to our next summit together.

I am grateful for my brother, Bill Ransdell, who showed me what the discipline and hard work of the pursuit of excellence really looks like up close. You continue to inspire me to be a better father and man.

I am grateful for my brother, Craig Feinberg, who has created incredible opportunities for me to pursue The Vertical in exotic destinations. You've shown me that with courage, there are incredible places in the world to be experienced, and I've enjoyed every moment in the mountains with you.

I am grateful for all my family who have enthusiastically believed in me, cheered me on and listened to my tall tales: Pam, Lisa, Deidre, and Laurel, Ted, Craig Wallace, Andy Wallace, Bill and Jeanie Ransdell, all of my step brothers and sisters, and all of my aunts, uncles, nieces, nephews, and cousins.

I am grateful for all those who've helped me along my journey to share my Vertical Lessons with the world: Michael Segura for always believing in me and investing in me. Dave Finnegan, Tina Klocke, Darlene Elder, Brian Vent, and Maxine Clark for supporting my adventures inside and outside of Build-A-Bear. For Mark Aubuchon, Rosemary Wilson and everyone in my Toastmasters family.

I am grateful for my team of speakers and coaches that helped me build significant momentum early in my speaking career: Karen Purves, Lloyd Abernathy, Emi Dielman, Mark Vickers, Sherry Prindle, Rob and Mary Hambleton, Jaime Swindell, Barrie Rhind, Robin White, John Ryan, Sharon Tick, MeChell Rentfro, Jaime Laudermilk, Lloyd Kirk, and Fred Pryor.

Thank you DJ at the Crowne Plaza Memphis for believing in me, a total stranger. You've been the light I need on days when I've been lost in the shadows.

I am grateful for my HDI family: Deborah Monroe, John Custy, Eddie Vidal, Mary Cruse, Julie Mohr, Rick Joslin, Sandy Seroskie, LaDonna Sprague, Michelle Steenhoek, Christina Montoya, Chris Farver, Jill Zimmerman, Mike Kublin, Katherine Lord, Deb Kowal, Randy Celaya, Fancy Mills, Jillian Bates, Christy Werth, Allyson Rollins, Leslie Cook, Jim and Debbie Bolton, Virginia Scuderi, Rae Ann Bruno, Beth Hagget, and Darien Chimoff.

Thank you for having me On Belay Sam Silverstein, Jessica Pettitt, Chris Clarke-Epstein, Laurie Ferrendelli, Shep Hyken, and Yossi Ghinsberg. I appreciate your direct influence, effort and inspiration. When I wanted to climb the easier route, you pushed me to dig deeper and climb higher. With your friendship I find myself celebrating this summit, looking forward to the next, grateful to be climbing with you.

I am grateful for my National Speakers Association (NSA) family, especially those who've gone above and beyond in their investment and belief in me: Jason Young, Carol Wiseman, Doug Devitre, Scott Ginsberg, Lois Creamer, Jeremy Epperson, Lethia Owens, Steve Hughes, Mary Kutheis, Cathy Sexton, Craig Valentine, Darren LaCroix, Guy Burns, Ed Tate, Patricia Fripp, Jeremy Tracey, Ed Rigsbee, Rory Vadon, Michael Davis, Bob Mohl, Bob Goodyear, Brian Walters, Jamey French, Scott McKain, David Newman, Steve Rizzo, Teresa Dukes, Rob Waldo Waldman, Nic Bittle, Jeff Salz, Tim Gard, Chris West, Gregg Gregory, Phil Gerbyshak, Deidre Van Nest, Mike Dilbeck, Jon Petz, Eliz Greene, Tony Alessandra, Jill Konrath, Patrick Almond, Mike Rayburn, Margaret Reynolds, Mark Sanborn, John Mayfield, Connie Podesta, Rob Bell, Karen Hoffman, Roger Courville, Robert Bradford, Judson Laipply, Matt Booth, Sean Carroll, Scott Cooksey, Laurie Guest, Bob Phibbs, Kelly Swanson, David Dye, Randy Gage, Dawnna St. Louis, Ascanio Pignatelli, Neen James, Thom Singer, Mark and Sue Scharenbroich, Eric Chester, Ron Karr, Jan Foxx, Sam Richter, Brad Montgomery, Dan Thurmon, Gerry O'brien, Andy Masters, Jeremy Flagg, Carl Potter, Jeffrey Ferrazzo, Karen Jacobson, Delatorro McNeal II, Chad Hymas, Chris Robinson, Patrick Maurer, Carey Lohrenz, Jason Hewlett, and all my NSA XY crew.

I am grateful for Maru Diaz and Julie Foote for believing in me and *Vertical Lessons*. Thank you for your commitment to helping us reach more people with our work.

I am grateful for everyone at Indie Books International for their belief in me and this book. Thank you Henry, Vikki, and Devin DeVries for pushing us to the summit. I am grateful to Denise Montgomery for your commitment to editing the mess of a mountain I handed to you in to what you hold in your hands today.

I am grateful for Mark LeBlanc. Your friendship and belief in me goes beyond your endless wisdom and guidance for my business and life. Thank you for being On Belay from the first time I met you.

I am grateful for my incredible son, Manley version 3.0. Your resilience, confidence, and love never ceases to amaze me. I cherish every moment of your amazing life and our incredible adventures yet to be.

I am grateful for my amazing daughter, Lizzy. Your passion, fire for life, and endless love for others lights me up. Our time together in the mountains and experiencing life are a blessing that always leaves me looking forward to the next.

I am grateful for my beautiful wife Emily. Without you, I'm convinced none of this would have happened. You truly are the secret to my summits, always On Belay. You and our wonderful children you gave life to have supported and believed in me on my darkest days, lighting the way for me when I was lost. With your unconditional love, I feel like the sun never sets and we can do anything we dream of. I cannot wait for our next summit together.

I am grateful to God for grace, love, and this extraordinary planet to experience. Thank you for the opportunity to serve and receive the love and light of so many people on my earthly expedition.

Tuolumne Meadows, July 14, 2016
Yosemite National Park, California

Manley, Emily, Manley version 3.0 and Lizzy on Cathedral Peak,
Yosemite National Park, California, July 18ᵗʰ, 2016

Enhance Your Experience

I invite you to visit ReachingYourNextSummit.com for free resources, full color photos and video to enrich your experience with this book.

- Access to free content updates, templates and exercises
- Vertical Lessons Strategic Summary PDF
- Full color photos and videos

Visit ReachingYourNextSummit.com

Get On Belay with Manley:
Human Voice: 314-724-3443
Manley@VerticalLessons.com

Manley Feinberg II
Vertical Lessons, Inc.
816 Aldan Dr.
St. Louis, MO. 63132

BOOK MANLEY TO SPEAK

Are you looking for an engaging and meaningful way to kick off or close your annual meeting or event?

Manley's unforgettable keynote programs will equip you with content you can use immediately, and also inspire you to actually step up with more focus, more commitment, and more momentum when you walk out the door. Regardless of your title, Manley's Vertical Lessons will help you build stronger relationships, develop more engaged teams, and lead with courage to realize greater results in your work and life.

"Best keynote speaker I've ever heard!"
Tom Moen,
Solutions Specialist, Microsoft

"Manley inspired and equipped our sales and marketing teams to achieve breakthrough Q3 / Q4 results. His message and content were customized and relevant so that it inspired my team to put it into action. His content is based on real results he's achieved in business— not theory. We enjoyed him so much, that we immediately re-hired him to work with more of our teams across the whole company."
Jim Norton, EVP Sales & Marketing, Bomgar

"Manley inspired and connected to our June 2015 audience of Energizer global leaders. The preparation by Manley to learn about our company in order to customize his message made a huge difference. I would highly recommend Manley as an inspirational speaker for leadership events.

Sue Drath, VP Global Rewards, Energizer

Get On Belay with Manley today to start a conversation on how a custom program can help you Reach Your Next Summit:

Human Voice: 314-724-3443

Info@VerticalLessons.com

Manley delivering a keynote leadership program to executives in Oregon, 2016

DEDICATION

This book is dedicated to Craig and Rich. You were two of the most incredible partners in The Vertical and beyond that anyone could ever dream of.

I am eternally grateful for every minute that my life was blessed with your friendship. The days burned brighter. I smiled bigger. I laughed harder. I am a better man for knowing you both.

CRAIG SIMS - SEPTEMBER 14TH, 1959 – SEPTEMBER 10TH, 2009

Craig Sims biking in Jackson Hole, Wyoming, July 1992 on his honeymoon with his love Vicki. Photo by Vicki Sims.

RICH COPELAND – SEPTEMBER 22ND, 1963 – MAY 18TH, 2014

Rich Celebrating the Summit of El Capitan, September 2011.
Photo by Ammon McNeely.

May we all strive to leave a legacy as significant as yours.

You are both forever On Belay in my heart and mind-
see you on The Summit dear friends.